Safari Crafts
FOR KIDS

**Includes Projects for Children
from Preschool to Sixth Grade:**

Colorful projects with an African theme!

Reproducible Awards and Certificates.

Bible Memory Verse Coloring Posters.

COMPILED BY KIM SULLIVAN

Gospel Light

How to make clean copies from this book.

You may make copies of portions of this book with a clean conscience if:

- you (or someone in your organization) are the original purchaser;
- you are using the copies you make for a non-commercial purpose (such as teaching or promoting a ministry) within your church or organization;
- you follow the instructions provided in this book.

However, it is illegal for you to make copies if:

- you are using the material to promote, advertise or sell a product or service other than for ministry fund-raising;
- you are using the material in or on a product for sale;
- you or your organization are **not** the original purchaser of this book.

By following these guidelines you help us keep our products affordable.
Thank you,
Gospel Light

Library of Congress Cataloging-in-Publication Data applied for

William T. Greig, Publisher
Dr. Elmer L. Towns, Senior Consulting Publisher
Billie Baptiste, Publisher, Research, Planning and Development
Christy Weir, Senior Editor
Kim Sullivan, Assistant Editor
Linda Bossoletti, Editorial Coordinator
Linda Crisp, Noni Pendleton, Loreen Robertson, Kim Sullivan, Contributing Writers
Joy Crouch, Sheryl Haystead, Kathleen McIntosh, Barbara Morris, Noni Pendleton, Jan Worsham, Contributing Editors
Carolyn Thomas, Designer
Chizuko Yasuda, Illustrator

© 1996 Gospel Light, Ventura, California 93006. All rights reserved. Printed in U.S.A.

Contents

Introduction to *Safari Crafts for Kids*

Safari Fun

In Swahili, *safari* means "journey." An African safari is an exciting adventure, but the most important journey we can begin is the adventure of knowing God as our Father through prayer. Children communicate naturally with their Father in heaven. This resource book is designed to encourage children to talk with God daily and reinforces that God is never too busy to listen to our prayers. God loves and cares for His children.

In addition to teaching about prayer you will also find a variety of African and safari-theme crafts. Your students will learn about the people, animals and customs of Africa while expressing their creativity. We hope that you and your students will enjoy your journey through Africa as you complete projects from *Safari Crafts for Kids*.

Personalize It!

We encourage you to use *Safari Crafts for Kids* as a basis for your craft program. You, as the teacher, parent or craft leader, play an essential role in leading enjoyable and successful craft projects for your children.

Feel free to alter the craft materials and instructions to suit your children's needs. Consider what materials you have on hand, what materials are available in your area and what materials you can afford to purchase. In some cases you will be able to substitute materials to use something you already have.

In addition, don't feel confined to the crafts in a particular age-level section. You may want to adapt a craft for younger and older age levels.

Three Steps to Success

What can you do to make sure craft time is successful and fun for your students? First, encourage creativity in each child! Remember, the process of creating is just as important as the final product. Provide a variety of materials with which children may work. Allow children to make choices on their own. Don't expect every child's project to turn out the same. Don't insist that children "stay in the lines."

Second, choose projects that are appropriate for the skill level of your students. Children become easily discouraged when a project is too difficult for them. Keep your children's skill level in mind when choosing craft projects. Finding the right projects for your students will increase the likelihood that all will be successful and satisfied with their finished products.

Finally, show an interest in the unique way each child approaches a project. Affirm the choices he or she has made. Treat each child's final product as a "masterpiece"!

The comments you give a child today can affect the way he or she views art in the future—so make it positive! Remember—the ability to create is part of being made in the image of God, the Creator!

Zungumza

Each craft in this book includes a very important section entitled *Zungumza*, which means "converse" in Swahili. These sections are designed to help you enhance craft times with thought-provoking conversation that is age-appropriate. The "Zungumza" section for a project may relate to prayer or it may include interesting facts about Africa. If your crafts program includes large groups of children, you may want to share these conversation suggestions with each helper who can in turn use them with individuals or small groups.

Craft Symbols

Many of the craft projects in *Safari Crafts for Kids* are appropriate for more than one age level. Next to the title of certain projects in this book you'll find the symbol shown below. This symbol tells what projects are suitable or adaptable for all elementary-age children—first through sixth grades. As you select projects, consider the particular children you are working with. Feel free to use your own ideas to make projects simpler or more difficult depending on the needs of your students.

In addition, some craft projects in this book require less preparation than others. The symbol shown below tells which projects require minimal preparation.

5

Crafts with a Message

Many of the projects in *Safari Crafts for Kids* can easily become crafts with a message. Children can create slogans or poetry as part of their projects. Or, you may want to provide photocopies of an appropriate poem, thought or Bible verse for children to attach to their crafts. Below are some examples of ways to use verses and drawings to enhance the craft projects in this book.

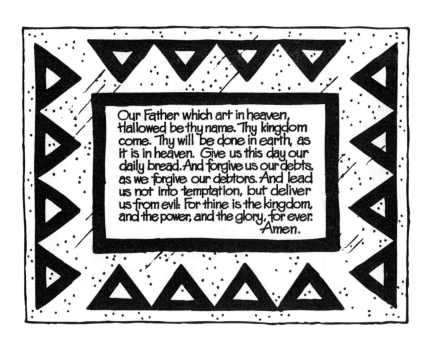

Be Prepared

If you are planning to use crafts with a child at home, here are three helpful tips:

■ Focus on the crafts in the book designated for your child's age, but don't ignore projects that are listed for older or younger ages. Elementary-age children enjoy many of the projects geared for preschool and kindergarten children. And younger children are always interested in doing "big kid" things. Just plan on working along with the child, helping with tasks the child can't handle alone.

■ Start with projects that call for materials you have around the house. Make a list of the items you do not have that are needed for projects you think your child will enjoy. Plan to gather those supplies in one expedition.

■ If certain materials seem too difficult to obtain, a little thought can usually lead to appropriate substitutions. And often the homemade version ends up being an improvement over the original plan.

If you are planning to lead a group of children in doing craft projects, keep these hints in mind:

■ Choose projects that will allow children to work with a variety of materials.

■ Make your selection of all projects far enough in advance to allow time to gather all needed supplies in one coordinated effort. Many projects use some of the same items.

■ Make up a sample of each project to be sure the directions are fully understood and potential problems can be avoided. **You may want to adapt some projects to simplify procedures or vary the materials required.**

■ Many items can be acquired as donations from people or businesses if you plan ahead and make your needs known. Many churches distribute lists of materials needed to their congregations and community and are able to provide crafts at little or no cost. Some items can be brought by the children themselves.

■ In making your supplies list, distinguish between items that every individual child will need and those that will be shared among a group.

■ Keep in mind that some materials may be shared among more than one age level, but only if there is good coordination between the groups. It is extremely frustrating for a teacher to expect to have scissors, only to discover another group is using them. Basic supplies that are used repeatedly in craft projects should usually be provided to every group.

Helpful Hints

Using Glue with Young Children

Since preschoolers have difficulty using glue bottles effectively, you may want to try one of the following procedures. Purchase glue in large containers (up to one gallon size).

a. Pour small amount of glue into several shallow containers (such as margarine tubs or the bottoms of soda bottles).

b. Dilute glue by mixing a little water into each container.

c. Children use paste brushes to spread glue on project.

OR

a. Pour a small amount of glue into a plastic margarine tub.

glue level

b. Give each child a cotton swab. The child dips the cotton swab into the glue and rubs glue on project.

swabs

c. Excess glue can be poured back into the large container at the end of each session.

Cutting with Scissors

When cutting with scissors is required for these crafts, take note of the fact that some of the children in your class may be left-handed. It is very difficult for a left-handed person to cut with scissors that were designed to be used with the right hand. Have available in your classroom two or three pairs of left-handed scissors. These can be obtained from a school supply center.

Using Acrylic Paints

Acrylic paints are required for many of the wood projects. Our suggestions are:

■ Provide smocks or old shirts for your children to wear, as acrylics may stain clothes.

■ Acrylics can be expensive for a large group of children. To make paint go further, squeeze a small amount into a shallow container and add water until mixture has a creamy consistency. Or you may use acrylic house paints.

■ Fill shallow containers with soapy water. Clean paintbrushes before switching colors and immediately after finishing project.

Section One/Prekindergarten-Kindergarten

Crafts for Young Children

Craft projects for young children are a blend of, "I wanna do it myself!" and "I need help!" Each project, because it is intended to come out looking like a recognizable something, usually requires a certain amount of adult assistance—in preparing a pattern, in doing some cutting, in preselecting magazine pictures, in tying a knot, etc. The younger the child, the more the adult will need to do, but care must always be taken not to rob the child of the satisfaction of his or her own unique efforts. Neither must the adult's desire to have a nice finished project override the child's pleasure at experimenting with color and texture. Avoid the temptation to do the project for the child or to improve on the child's efforts.

Some of the crafts have enrichment and simplification ideas included with them. An enrichment idea provides a way to make the craft more challenging for the older child. A simplification idea helps the younger child complete the craft more successfully. If you find a child frustrated with some of the limitations of working on a structured craft—although most of the projects in this book allow plenty of leeway for children to be themselves—it may be a signal the child needs an opportunity to work with more basic, less structured materials: blank paper and paints, play dough, or abstract collages (gluing miscellaneous shapes or objects onto surfaces such as paper, cardboard or anything else to which glue will adhere). Remember the cardinal rule of thumb in any task a young child undertakes: The process the child goes through is more important than the finished product.

Binoculars

(15-20 MINUTES)

Materials: Black, olive green or grey acrylic spray paint, yarn, permanent felt pens, safari animal stickers, hole punch, craft glue, scissors, newspaper, measuring stick. For each child—two toilet paper tubes, one paper clip.

Preparation: In well-ventilated area, cover ground with newspaper and spray paint tubes. Let dry. Cut yarn into 2-foot (60-cm) lengths—one for each child.

Instruct each child in the following procedures:

■ Spread glue lengthwise down the outside of one tube and press tubes together (see sketch). Secure tubes together with paper clip to allow glue to dry (see sketch).

■ With teacher's help, punch one hole in outer edge of each tube (see sketch).

■ With teacher's help tie one end of yarn piece through each hole.

■ Decorate tubes with stickers and felt pens. Remove paper clips when glue has dried.

Enrichment Idea: Children use rubber bands to attach pieces of colored cellophane over ends of binoculars.

Zungumza: What has God made that you can see through your binoculars? God made lots of things for us to see. When we pray, we can thank God for what He has made.

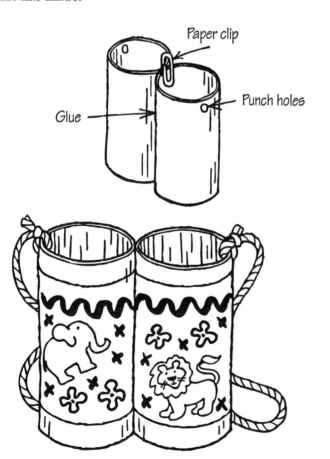

Paper clip

Glue

Punch holes

Safari Souvenir Book

(15-20 MINUTES)

Materials: Felt in a variety of colors, wide-tip permanent felt pen, craft glue, stapler and staples, scissors, ruler. For each child—five resealable plastic sandwich bags, several flat nature items (leaves, flowers, small pebbles, etc.).

Preparation: Cut felt into 7x12-inch (17.5x30-cm) rectangles—one for each child. Cut additional felt into a variety of small triangles and squares, about 1 inch (2.5 cm) in size. Fold each felt piece in half. Use felt pen to letter "Things God Made" on front half of each felt piece (sketch b).

Instruct each child in the following procedures:

■ Lay sandwich bags directly on top of one another with openings facing same direction.

■ Staple bags together at sides opposite of zip-lock openings (sketch a).

■ Lay bags inside the folded felt cover, stapled edge next to the fold. Staple all layers together (sketch b).

■ Glue felt shapes around the edge of book to make a border (sketch c).

■ Fill bags with nature items.

Enrichment Idea: Take children on a nature walk to collect items for their books, or give them items they might see on a safari (fake fur, a feather, sand, leaves) to put in their books.

Zungumza: What has God made, (Jessica)? We can learn about God by looking at the wonderful things He makes. We can also learn about God by listening to the stories Jesus told us in the Bible.

a.

Nature objects inside bags

Plastic bags with zip-lock openings

Felt

b.

c.

Things God Made

Things God Made

Staples

Long-Neck Giraffe
(15-20 MINUTES)

Materials: Giraffe Pattern, yellow card stock, photocopier, brown yarn, brown crayons or felt pens, pencil, glue, scissors, ruler. For each child—two wooden clothespins (spring-type).

Preparation: Photocopy Giraffe Pattern onto card stock—one for each child. Cut yarn into 2-inch (5-cm) lengths—one for each child. (*Optional:* Cut card stock into 5x9-inch (12.5x22.5-cm) rectangles—one for each child. Trace giraffe pattern onto each card stock rectangle.)

Instruct each child in the following procedures:
- Cut out giraffe.
- Color brown spots on giraffe's body and neck.
- Glue yarn in place for tail.
- With teacher's help, fold giraffe's neck accordion-style as in sketch.
- Clip clothespins onto bottom of giraffe's body to make legs.

Simplification: Teacher cuts out the giraffes for younger children.

Zungumza: **Giraffes have long necks. Why do you think God made their necks so long?** (To eat the leaves at the top of tall trees.) **What do we use our necks for?** (Children respond.) **We can use our necks to bow our heads when we pray. When we bow our heads to God, we show Him that we think He is very important— just like a King!**

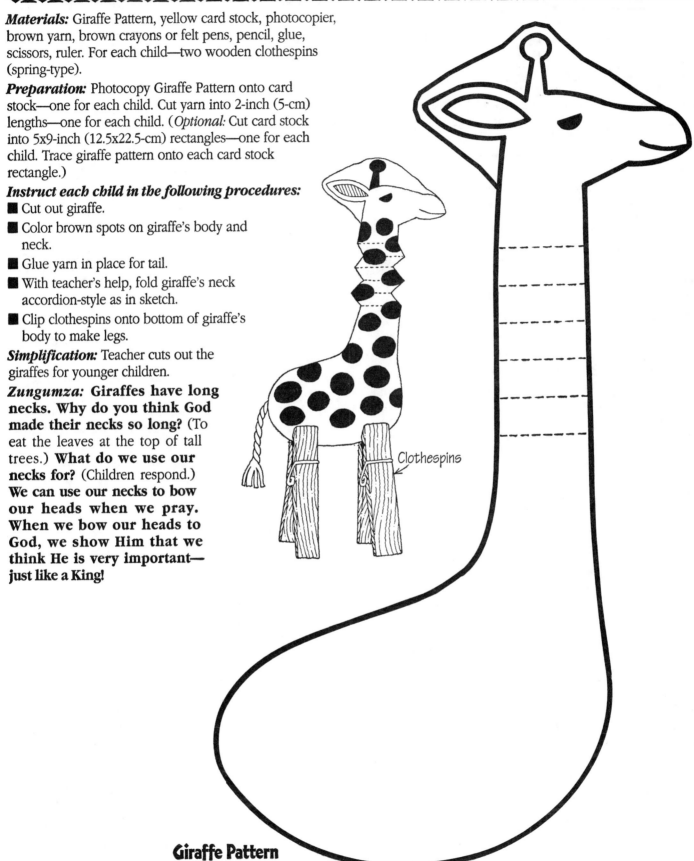

Clothespins

Giraffe Pattern

Praise Shaker

(15-20 MINUTES)

Materials: White construction paper, cardboard, dried beans, crayons, liquid tempera paints, paintbrushes, shallow containers, glue, scissors, newspaper. For each child—one tennis ball canister or potato chip canister with lid, one tree leaf.

Preparation: Cut construction paper to fit around each canister. Cut cardboard into squares larger than a leaf—one for each child. Glue smooth side of each leaf onto cardboard square and allow glue to dry (sketch a). Cover work area with newspaper.

Instruct each child in the following procedures:

■ Spread a thin coat of paint onto leaf.

■ Place construction paper on painted side of leaf and press heavily. Carefully lift paper (sketch b).

■ Repeat printing process several times to make a design. Let dry.

■ Place several beans inside canister and glue on plastic lid.

■ Glue decorated paper onto canister (sketch c).

Enrichment Idea: Older children can glue leaves onto cardboard to make their own printing blocks.

Zungumza: **In Africa, children love to make music and sing to God just like we do. They tell Him they love Him and thank Him for taking care of them. This is called praising God. You can use your Praise Shaker when you sing songs to God.**

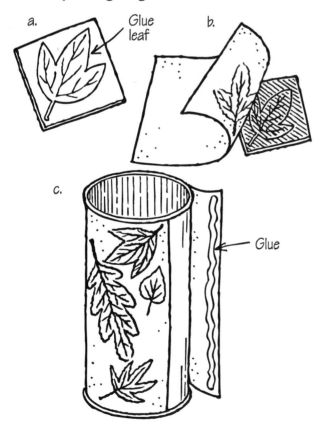

Paw Print Paperweight

(15-20 MINUTES)

Materials: Acrylic paints, sponges, shallow containers, felt, scissors, glue, clear acrylic spray, ruler, baby wipes for cleanup, newspaper. For each child—one smooth 3- to 4-inch (7.5- to 10-cm) stone.

Preparation: Cut sponges into 1-inch (2.5-cm) circles. Cut felt into 2-inch (5-cm) squares—one for each child. Cover work area with newspaper. Pour paint into shallow containers.

Instruct each child in the following procedures:

■ Glue the felt piece to the bottom of the stone.

■ Dip the sponge into the paint and print a circle on the stone.

■ Dip finger into the paint and make four fingerprints around one side of the printed circle (see sketch).

■ Print more paw prints on stone if space allows.

■ Clean fingers with baby wipes.

■ When paint is dry, teacher sprays stones with clear acrylic spray to seal.

Zungumza: **Have you ever made a hand print or footprint in mud? Have you ever seen an animal paw print in the mud or in the dirt? God gave lions and cheetahs paws so they can climb in trees. He made zebras and giraffes with hooves, so they can run fast over rocks. God gave us hands and feet so we can do lots of things. What can you do with your hands? with your feet?**

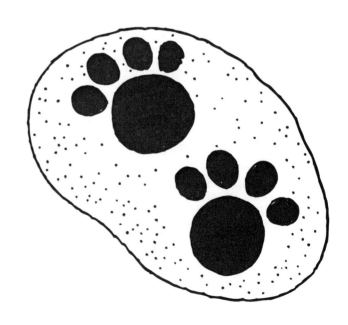

Daily Bread Magnet
(25-30 MINUTES)

Materials: Ribbon Patterns, Bread Pattern, photocopier, clear acrylic spray, scissors, glue, ruler, construction paper, black yarn. For each child—one slice of mini-toast (found in cracker or deli sections of most grocery stores), two wiggle eyes, one ½-inch (1.25-cm) round magnet. **Note:** Sliced mini-loaves of bread may be used when toasted in a 350° oven until hard.

Preparation: Photocopy Bread and Ribbon Patterns onto construction paper-one for each child. Cut yarn into 1-inch (2.5-cm) pieces—one for each child. Spray toast with clear acrylic spray.

Instruct each child in the following procedures:
- Glue wiggle eyes to toast.
- Glue on yarn to make smile.
- Cut out bread pattern.
- Glue toast to bread cutout (sketch a).
- Cut out ribbon patterns.
- Glue magnet to back of bread cutout (make sure glue is applied to repellent side, not magnetic side).
- Glue ribbons to back of bread cutout (sketch b).

Simplification: For younger children, teacher cuts out construction paper patterns.

Zungumza: The Bible says God will give us the things we need to grow. We can pray to God and say, "Give us this day our daily bread." What are some other things that God has given to you? (Family, friends, pets.) **Your Daily Bread magnet can remind you to thank God for the people who care for you and the things He has given you.**

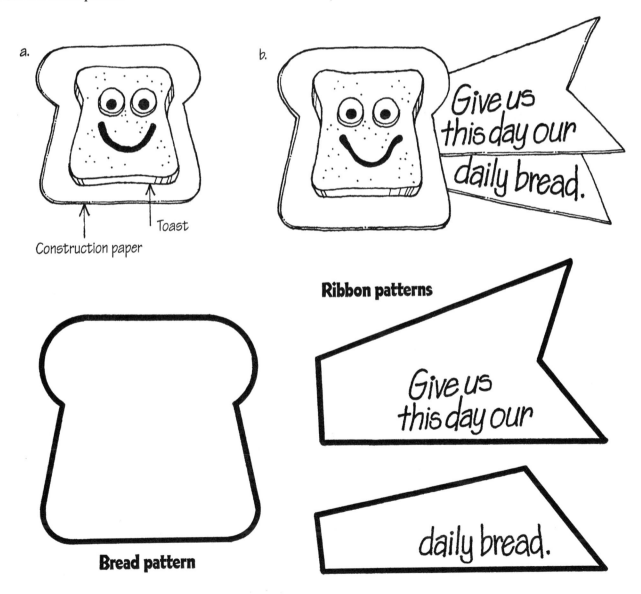

a.

Construction paper

Toast

b.

Give us this day our daily bread.

Ribbon patterns

Give us this day our

daily bread.

Bread pattern

Lion Mask

Materials: Nose Pattern, yellow and orange crepe paper streamers, glue sticks, stapler and staples, elastic string, black felt pens, yellow construction paper, pencils, scissors, ruler. For every two children—one yellow paper plate.

Preparation: Trace Nose Pattern onto yellow construction paper and cut out—one for each child. Cut a 3-inch (7.5-cm) circle from construction paper and cut in half—two halves for each child. Cut crepe paper streamers into 8-inch (20-cm) lengths—twelve for each child. Cut paper plates in half—one half for each child. Cut two eye holes in each plate as shown in sketch a. Cut elastic string into 12-inch (30-cm) lengths—one for each child. Tie a knot on each end of elastic lengths.

Instruct each child in the following procedures:

■ With teacher's help, staple ends of elastic onto sides of plate (sketch b).

■ Use glue stick to glue ends of streamers onto sides and top of paper plate as shown in sketch c.

■ Glue half circles onto top edge of paper plate for ears (sketch c).

■ Use felt pen to trace around eye holes.

■ Use felt pen to color in bottom portion of yellow nose piece (sketch d).

■ With teacher's help, fold nose in half lengthwise. Glue edges of nose between eye holes (sketch e). Hold in place while glue dries.

Enrichment Idea: Use different colors of plates and marking pens to create a variety of safari animals.

Zungumza: What sound does a lion make? (Children respond.) **God gave the lion a special way to talk to other lions. Each animal has its own special way to talk. God gave us our voices to talk to our friends and our family. God also wants us to talk to Him. He hears our prayers wherever we are.**

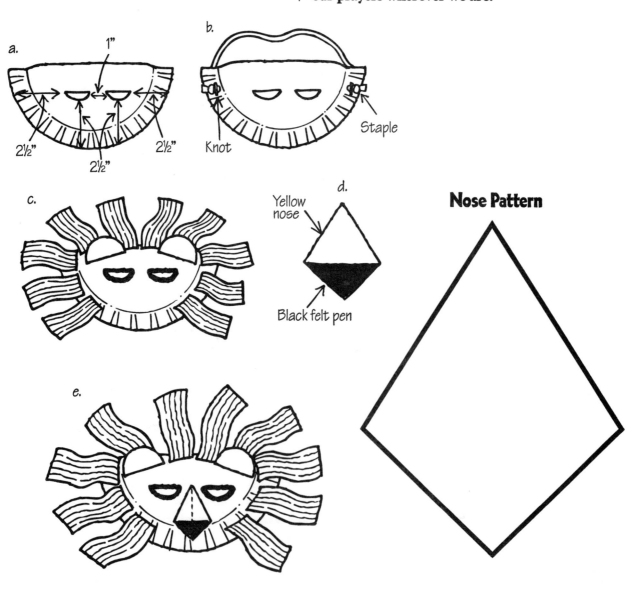

a. 1" 2½" 2½" 2½"

b. Knot Staple

c.

d. Yellow nose Black felt pen

Nose Pattern

e.

African Sunset Jar

Materials: Table salt, spray paint, brown, orange, red and blue powdered tempera paint, measuring utensils, cotton balls, spoons, five plastic margarine tubs with lids, newspaper. For each child—one clean baby food jar with lid. **Optional**—yellow fabric paint squeeze bottle.

Preparation: Spray paint jar lids. In margarine tubs, mix 1 cup (.24 l) salt with 1 tsp. (5 ml) tempera for each color. In addition to the four tempera colors, mix a light tan color by using less brown tempera. (Five cups of salt will fill 10 baby food jars.) Place spoon in each container of colored salt. Cover work area with newspaper.

Instruct each child in the following procedures:

- With spoon, layer brown and tan salt in bottom of baby food jar (sketch a).
- Layer red and orange salt to make sunset.
- Add blue layer near the top of the sunset.
- When filled, tap jar to let salt settle.
- Place several cotton balls on top of salt. Tightly screw on lid.

Enrichment Idea: Have children help mix tempera and salt. Measure ingredients, snap lid on margarine tubs and have them shake the mixture to color the salt. With fabric paint, children paint a sun setting on the jar after it is filled and sealed.

Zungumza: What colors are in your sunset? God puts all those colors together in the sky every evening. He has made beautiful things for us to see, touch, smell and hear. What are your favorite things that God has made?

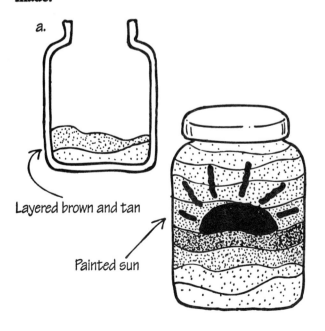

a.

Layered brown and tan

Painted sun

African Mud Mats

Materials: Soil, wire mesh strainer or window screen, brown and blue liquid tempera paint, measuring cups, small coffee cans, shallow trays, animal-shaped sponges, paint-stirring sticks, heavyweight muslin, pinking shears, measuring stick, newspaper.

Preparation: Gather 1 cup (.24 l) dry soil for every four children in class. With pinking shears, cut muslin into 12x18-inch (30x45-cm) mats. Cover work area with newspaper.

Instruct each child in the following procedures:

- Divide class into groups of four. With adult help, children take turns shaking 1 cup (.24 l) soil through wire screen into coffee can until they have ½ cup (.12 l) fine soil.
- Add ¼ cup (.06 l) paint to fine dirt and stir until smooth. (Add a small amount of water if mixture seems too dry or becomes dry while sponging.)
- Pour paints into shallow trays.
- Dip animal sponges into paint and press onto mat.
- Let dry overnight.

Zungumza: **In Africa, it gets very hot. Many African animals like to go to a mud hole to cool off. Hippos like to swim in the muddy water. Other animals keep cool by lying in the mud. How do you like to keep cool in the summer?**

Lion Puzzle Magnet

(15-20 MINUTES)

Materials: Lion Pattern, yellow poster board, pencil, small jigsaw puzzle pieces, brown and orange spray paint, black felt pens, 4-inch (10-cm) magnet strips, craft glue, scissors, newspaper, one plastic milk jug lid. For each child—two 7-mm wiggle eyes.

Preparation: In well-ventilated area, cover ground with newspaper. Spray paint puzzle pieces orange and brown—approximately 12 total pieces for each child. Trace and cut out Lion Pattern—one for each child. Using plastic lid as a pattern, draw a circle for the face of each poster board lion (sketch a). Cut magnet strips into 3-inch (7.5-cm) lengths—one for each child. Cut triangular tips off some puzzle pieces to use for lion tail—one tip for each child (sketch b).

Instruct each child in the following procedures:

■ Glue wiggle eyes on the lion's face.

■ With felt pen, draw nose, mouth, whiskers, toes and tail.

■ Glue puzzle pieces around face to make mane.

■ Glue triangular tip on end of tail.

■ Glue a magnet strip to back.

Simplification Idea: Teacher draws lion face and toes or photocopies Lion Pattern onto yellow card stock.

Zungumza: The lion is called the "King of Beasts" because he is so strong and powerful. God is also called a King. He is even stronger and more powerful than the lion. He made the world and everything in it. He made you, me and the lion, too!

a.   Drawn circle

b.   Cut off triangular tips

Puzzle Pieces

Lion Pattern

Rhythm Drum

(15-20 MINUTES)

▼▲▼▲▼▲▼▲▼▲▼▲▼▲▼▲▼▲▼▲▼▲▼▲▼▲

Materials: Muslin fabric, brown wrapping paper, rubber bands, yarn in a variety of colors, wide felt-tip pens in a variety of colors, glue, scissors, ruler. For each child—one medium-size round metal canister with plastic lid (such as a powdered drink or roasted nuts container).

Preparation: Cut brown wrapping paper into rectangles large enough to cover each canister—one for each child. Cut muslin into 7-inch (17.5-cm) circles—one for each child.

Instruct each child in the following procedures:

■ Use pens to draw a colorful design on paper.

■ Glue paper around canister (sketch a).

■ Glue rim of plastic lid onto canister to secure lid in place.

■ Place muslin circle over plastic lid. Secure muslin with a rubber band (sketch b).

■ With teacher's help, cut and tie several lengths of yarn around rubber band (sketch c).

■ Use hands to beat a rhythm on drum.

Enrichment Idea: For a more authentic-looking drum, wrap wood-grain self-adhesive paper around container. To make bongo drums, secure two containers together with a large rubber band.

Zungumza: **Children in Africa sometimes enjoy making music to God. They beat drums and clap their hands. They sing and play instruments. When we make music to God, we are praising Him. We are telling God we're glad that He loves us!**

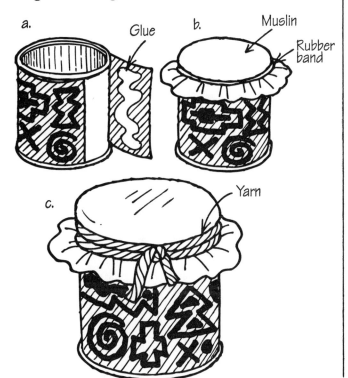

Safari Suitcase

(10 MINUTES)

▼▲▼▲▼▲▼▲▼▲▼▲▼▲▼▲▼▲▼▲▼▲▼▲▼▲

Materials: Cording, safari animal stickers (available in stationery stores or from Gospel Light), colored electrical tape, scissors, ruler. For each child—one rectangular plastic disposable baby wipe box with flip-up lid.

Preparation: Cut cording into 12-inch (30-cm) lengths—one for each child. Use tip of scissors to poke two holes in the top of each box as shown in sketch a. Cut tape in various lengths. Stick one end of each tape length to a table edge so children can easily retrieve tape.

Instruct each child in the following procedures:

■ Stick lengths of tape on the top, front and back of box to make a free form design or straps on a suitcase (sketch b).

■ Decorate box with stickers.

■ With teacher's help, thread cording through holes in box and tie a knot at each end on inside of lid (sketch c).

Zungumza: **There are many things that you can do with your suitcase. You can carry things that are special to you. You can use your suitcase to hold pictures that you make for God. You can even carry home the special things you make at VBS! What will you put in your suitcase, (Eric)?**

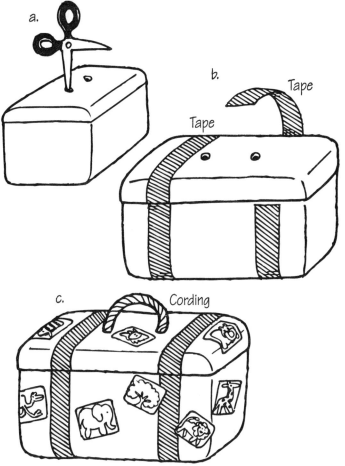

African "Beaded" Mirror
(20-30 MINUTES)

Materials: Poster board, uncooked salad macaroni, food coloring, measuring cup, small containers, cookie sheets, glue, pencils, scissors, waxed paper. For each child—one 2-inch (5-cm) round mirror, one chenille wire.

Preparation: Dye several different colors of macaroni. In each small container mix several drops of food coloring and about ½ cup (.12l) water. Drop uncooked macaroni into colored water. Soak for no longer than five minutes. Remove macaroni and spread on cookie sheets or waxed paper to dry. On poster board, make a circle pattern ½-inch (1.25-cm) larger than mirror. Use pattern to trace and cut poster board circles—one for each child.

Instruct each child in the following procedures:
- Glue mirror to center of poster board circle (sketch a).
- String macaroni on chenille wire. Lay chenille wire around edge of mirror to measure and add macaroni until ends meet at top.
- Twist ends of wire once at top of mirror, then again at ends of wire to form hanger (sketch b).
- Squeeze glue onto poster board around edge of mirror. Press wire with macaroni onto glue. Let dry.

Zungumza: In Africa, people make many beautiful things out of beads. They sew them on their clothing, decorate items like our mirror, and make jewelry. Africans use beads made out of glass, bones, shells and wood. They even make small beads out of grass that is woven together very tightly.

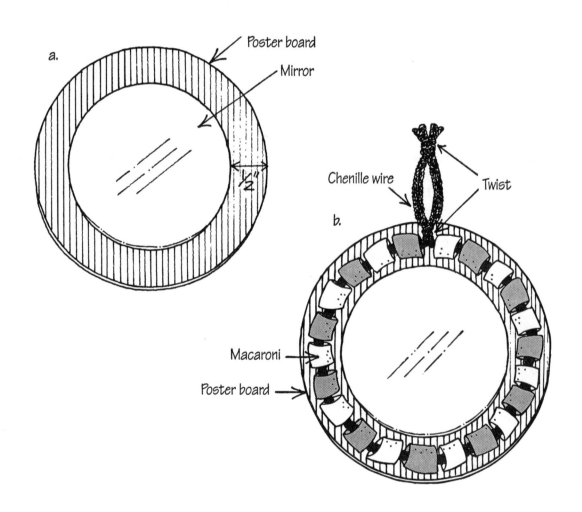

Elephant Feet

(20-25 MINUTES)

Materials: Foot Pattern, grey liquid tempera paint, paint-brushes, pink construction paper, glue, hole punch, craft knife, scissors, pencil, ruler, shallow containers, newspaper. For each child—two shoe boxes with lids (approximately the same size), one chenille wire.

Preparation: Cut pink construction paper into 1 ¾-inch (4.4-cm) circles—six for each child. Trace Foot Pattern onto top of each box lid (sketch a). Use craft knife to cut out shaded area as shown in pattern. Use craft knife to cut along the dotted lines. Punch holes in flaps where indicated on pattern. Cut chenille wires in half—two halves for each child. Cover work area with newspaper. Pour paint into shallow containers.

Instruct each child in the following procedures:
- Glue lid onto top of each box.
- Paint entire shoe box. Allow paint to dry.
- Glue pink circles onto front edge of box for elephant's toenails (sketch b).
- Insert a foot into each shoe box. Thread a chenille wire through holes in each box and twist tightly to secure boxes onto feet.
- Now do the Elephant Stomp!

Zungumza: Elephants have to stomp when they walk because their feet don't bend like our feet do. They can't jump like other animals. But God has made elephants really special. What makes elephants different from other animals?

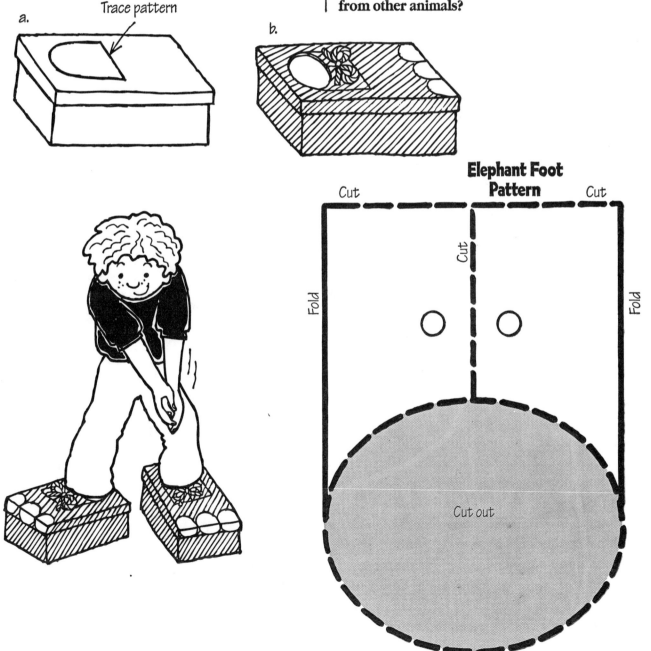

a. Trace pattern

b.

Elephant Foot Pattern
Cut — Cut — Cut

Fold — Fold

Cut out

19

Sunshine Mobile

(15-20 MINUTES)

Materials: Several magazines with a variety of pictures, large yellow paper plates, orange and yellow construction paper, fishing line, hammer, nail, wood scrap, permanent black felt pen, hole punch, glue, scissors, ruler. For each child—four frozen-juice can lids (any size).

Preparation: Cut paper plates in half—one half for each child. Cut fishing line into 12-inch (30-cm) lengths—five for each child. Cut construction paper into 2-inch (5-cm) squares, then cut in half to make triangles. Place juice can lids on scrap-wood surface. Use hammer and nail to make a hole at top of each lid (sketch a). Tie fishing line through hole in each lid. Look through magazines and tear out pages with small pictures of items that a child might be thankful for. With black pen, letter "Thank You, God, for..." along edge of paper plate (sketch b).

Instruct each child in the following procedures:

■ With teacher's help, punch four evenly-spaced holes along bottom edge of plate and one on top (sketch b).

■ Glue paper triangles around curved edge of paper plate.

■ Cut out magazine pictures of objects he or she is thankful for.

■ Glue pictures onto both sides of juice can lids.

■ With teacher's help, tie lids to plate (sketch b).

■ To make hanger, tie length of fishing line through hole on top.

Simplification: Eliminate paper triangles. For younger children, teacher cuts out small pictures from magazines.

Zungumza: What are you thankful for, (Andre)? God takes care of you. He helps you have what you need to grow up healthy and strong. We can tell God we are glad that He takes care of us. We can thank Him for our (family, pets, food, etc.) too.

Hippo Sun Visor
(15-20 MINUTES)

Materials: Hippo Ear Pattern, grey spray paint, self-adhesive paper hole reinforcements, white and grey construction paper, transparent tape, pencil, scissors, ruler, craft glue, newspapers. For each child—one child-size white plastic sun visor (available at craft stores), two 20-mm wiggle eyes.

Preparation: Cover an outside area with newspapers and spray visors with grey paint. Cut white construction paper into 1x1 ½-inch (2.5x3.75-cm) rectangles—two for each child. Trace Hippo Ear pattern onto grey construction paper and cut out—two for each child.

Instruct each child in the following procedures:

■ Fold one end of each paper rectangle (sketch a).

■ To make tusks, tape folded edges of white rectangles to the underside of the visor bill (sketch b).

■ Attach paper reinforcements on top of visor to make nostrils.

■ Glue grey paper ears onto side of visor band.

■ Glue wiggle eyes on visor band (sketch c).

Zungumza: A baby hippo often rides on its mother's back in the water. The baby gets wet and cool and the mother keeps it safe. Who keeps you safe? (Mother and father.) **God keeps us safe too. He always cares for us. We can pray to Him whenever we feel afraid. We can ask Him to help us.**

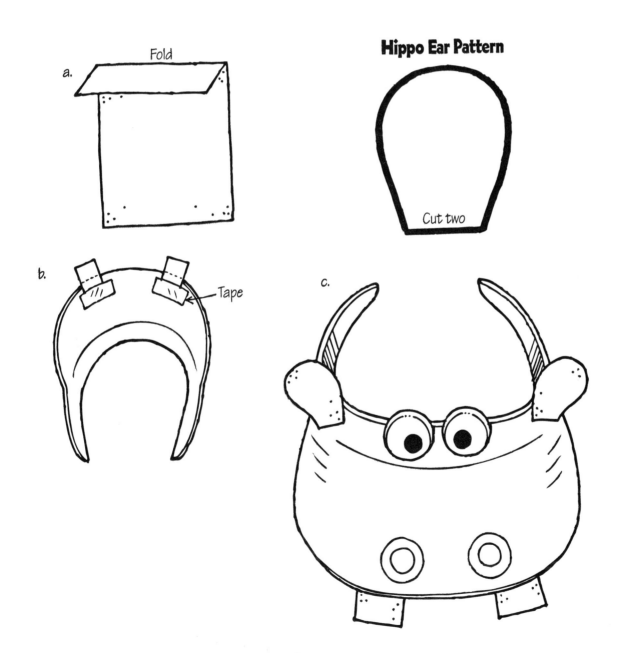

a. Fold

Hippo Ear Pattern

Cut two

b. Tape

c.

Elephant Treasure Box
(20-25 MINUTES)

Materials: Elephant Ear Pattern, grey acrylic paint, grey construction paper, paintbrushes, shallow containers, self-adhesive paper hole reinforcements, pen, glue, craft knife, scissors, ruler, newspaper. For each child—one half-gallon milk carton, two 20-mm wiggle eyes.

Preparation: Wash and dry milk cartons. Use craft knife to cut each carton as shown in sketch a. Use pen to trace ear pattern on each flap of cut milk carton. Cut out ears and round the head with scissors. Cut construction paper into 1x9-inch (2.5x22.5-cm) strips—one for each child. Cover work area with newspaper. Pour paint into shallow containers.

Instruct each child in the following procedures:
■ Paint the outside of the box.
■ Paint front and back of the elephant's head and ears. Allow paint to dry (sketch a).

■ Make elephant toenails by sticking paper reinforcements on bottom front edge of box—three for each foot (sketch b).
■ Fold construction paper strip accordion-style, leaving the last 1 inch (2.5 cm) unfolded.
■ Glue the unfolded end of the accordion trunk to the elephant's face (sketch c).
■ Glue on wiggle eyes.

Zungumza: Elephants are very strong and powerful animals. Sometimes people in Africa use elephants to carry heavy loads for them. They don't have cars or trucks to haul things. The elephant you made today can hold your special treasures. What will your elephant hold?

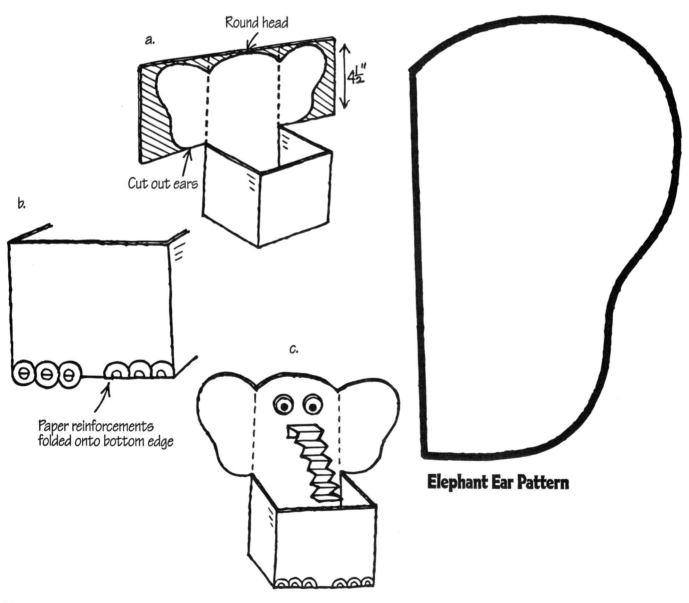

Round head

Cut out ears

$4\frac{1}{2}$"

a.

b.

Paper reinforcements folded onto bottom edge

c.

Elephant Ear Pattern

22

Zebra Print Necklace

(15-20 MINUTES)

Materials: White card stock or unlined index cards, pony beads, plastic lanyard, white plastic drinking straws, black ink pads (washable ink, if available), jar lids with ribbed edges (instant coffee or peanut butter lids), scissors, tape, hole puncher, butcher paper.

Preparation: Cut card stock or index cards into squares and triangles at least 1 inch (2.5 cm) in size. Cut straws into 1-inch (2.5-cm) lengths. Cut lanyard into 3-ft. (.9-m) lengths—one for each child. Cover tables with butcher paper.

Instruct each child in the following procedures:

■ Press ribbed edge of jar lid onto ink pad. Roll inked edge over card stock shapes to print zebra stripes (sketch a).

■ Turn shapes over and repeat printing.

■ With hole punch, punch one hole in the center of each shape.

■ Tape one end of lanyard length to keep beads from falling off when stringing (sketch b).

■ String zebra print shapes, beads and straw pieces onto lanyard to make necklace of his or her own design.

■ Remove tape from lanyard. With teacher's help, hold lanyard ends together and tie in a knot.

Simplification: For younger children, teacher punches holes in paper shapes.

Zungumza: **What colors are zebra stripes? Zebras have stripes so they can hide from animals that hunt them. When zebras are together in a herd it's hard to see just one zebra because all their stripes blend together. God gave them stripes to protect them. Who does God give to protect us?**

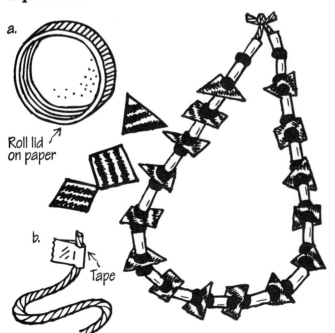

a.

Roll lid on paper

b.

Tape

Wildlife Park Picture

(20-25 MINUTES)

Materials: Large sheets of black construction paper, colored chalk (including brown, green and blue), aerosol hair spray, animal crackers, green netting, blue foil wrapping paper, small twigs, cotton balls, sand, shallow containers, several plastic spoons, scissors, glue.

Preparation: Cut netting and foil paper into a variety of small shapes and place on table. Pour sand into shallow containers. Place a spoon in each container of sand. Place animal crackers, cotton balls and twigs in separate containers.

Instruct each child in the following procedures:

■ Use chalk to color an African safari scene on black construction paper. Color blue sky. Color brown sand. Color green grass.

■ When completed, teacher sprays chalk picture with hair spray in well-ventilated area. Let dry.

■ Glue on twigs for tree trunks and green netting for foliage. Glue on pieces of blue foil paper for water and cotton balls for clouds.

■ Cover selected areas with glue and sprinkle on sand. With teacher's help, pour excess sand back into container.

■ Glue on animal crackers.

Zungumza: **Some parts of Africa are very hot, so the watering holes are full of lots of animals and birds. God made water for all the animals to drink. What animals are at your watering hole, (Michelle)?**

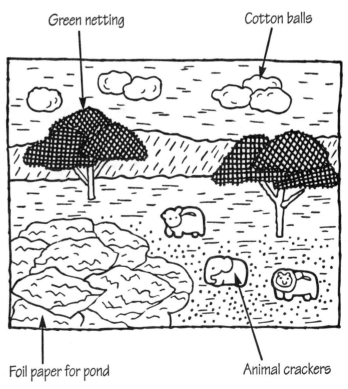

Green netting

Cotton balls

Foil paper for pond

Animal crackers

Flutter Butterfly

(20-25 MINUTES)

Materials: Flutter Butterfly Pattern, white paper, photocopier, thin tempera paints in squeeze bottles, wide felt pens, scissors, ruler, newspapers, glue. For each child—one tongue depressor, one-half black chenille wire, one spring-type clothespin, one drinking straw.

Preparation: Photocopy Flutter Butterfly Pattern onto paper—one for each child. Cut chenille wires in half. Cover work area with newspapers.

Instruct each child in the following procedures:

■ Cut out Flutter Butterfly Pattern.

■ Fold butterfly on the center fold line, then fold back on outer fold lines (sketch a). Lay paper with center fold pointing down.

■ With teacher's help, squeeze small drops of paint onto one butterfly wing.

■ With straw, blow paint drops to make designs. (Younger children may not know how to blow. Provide cotton swabs for them to spread paint drops.)

■ Press wings together to print painted wing on unpainted wing. Open wings and allow to dry.

■ Color both sides of tongue depressor with felt pen.

■ Fold chenille wire around tongue depressor at one end. Twist ends together to secure around tongue depressor. Spread apart and bend ends to make antennae (sketch b).

■ Glue tongue depressor inside fold of wings.

■ Clip clothespin to underneath side of butterfly.

■ Hold clothespin and move your hand up and down to make your butterfly flutter.

Simplification: Children use felt pens instead of paint to make designs on wings. For younger children, teacher cuts out Flutter Butterfly Pattern.

Zungumza: What colors did you use to paint your butterfly, (Tasia)? God made butterflies in many different colors and patterns. He made people with many different colors of eyes, hair and skin too. He loves us and He made us all special!

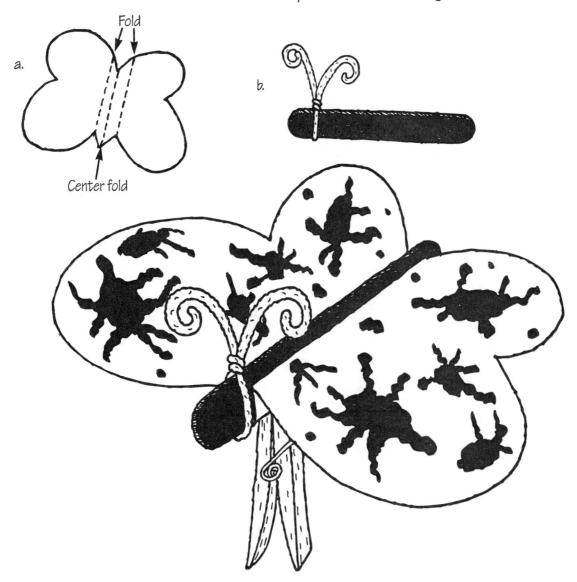

24

Flutter Butterfly Pattern

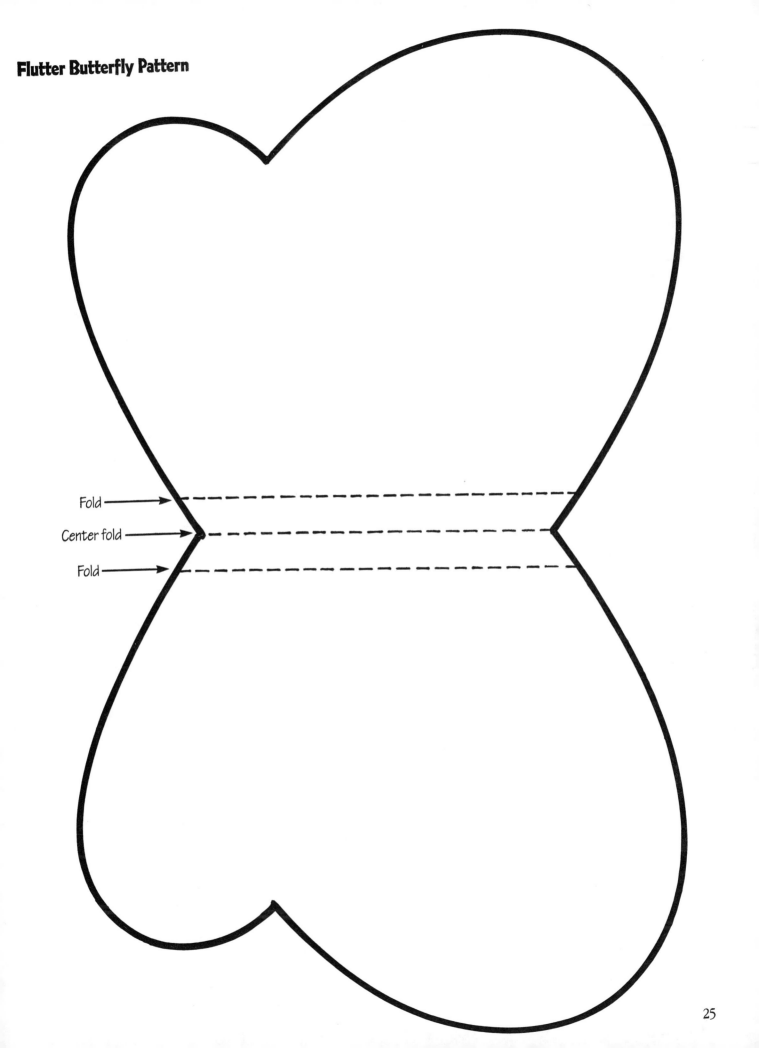

Fold →

Center fold →

Fold →

25

Lion Crayon Holder
(20-25 MINUTES)

Materials: Gold acrylic spray paint, yellow poster board, yellow construction paper, small corkscrew pasta (rotini), black felt pen, craft glue, pencil, scissors, ruler, newspaper. For each child—medium-size round can, two 20-mm wiggle eyes.

Preparation: Cut poster board into 5-inch (12.5-cm) circles—one for each child. Cut construction paper into rectangles large enough to wrap around each can—one for each child. Cover work area with newspaper. Spray paint pasta gold. Let dry.

Instruct each child in the following procedures:

■ Glue eyes onto yellow circle.

■ Use felt pen to draw nose and mouth of lion.

■ Glue ends of pasta around circle to make a mane (sketch c). Allow glue to dry.

■ Spread glue on construction paper and wrap around can (sketch b).

■ Glue head onto can (sketch c). Hold in place until glue is dry.

Zungumza: A male lion looks powerful with his furry mane around his face. But female lions are better hunters because they can run faster without a heavy mane. The fur around the male's head weighs him down. He can't run as fast as a female lion who has shorter fur.

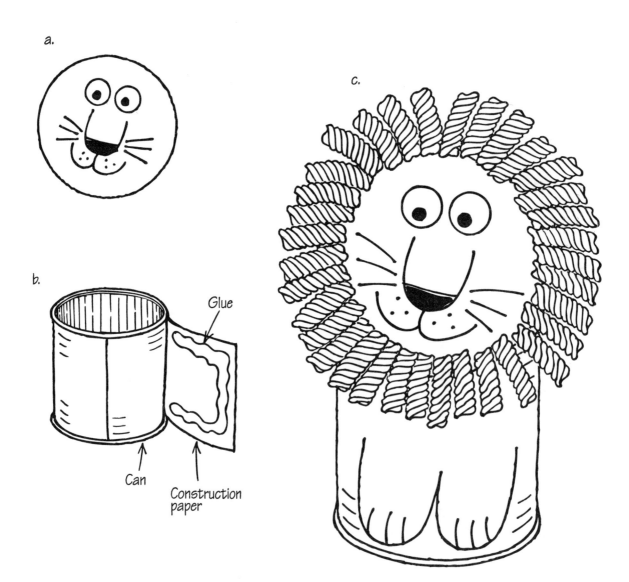

Section Two/Grades 1-3

Crafts for Younger Elementary

Children in the first few years of school delight in completing craft projects. They have a handle on most of the basic skills needed, they are eager to participate and their taste in art has usually not yet surpassed their ability to produce. In other words, they generally like the things they make.

Since reading ability is not a factor in most craft projects, crafts can be a great leveler in a group. Some children excel here who may or may not be top achievers in other areas.

Many of the projects in the section for young children also will appeal to younger elementary children.

Lord's Prayer Place Mat

(20-30 MINUTES)

Materials: Lord's Prayer Pattern, brown packaging paper or large grocery sacks, clear self-adhesive paper, tempera paints, objects to print with (such as vegetables or pieces of sponge), shallow containers, felt pens, measuring stick, scissors, glue, colored paper, photocopier, newspaper.

Preparation: Cut brown packaging paper into 11x15-inch (27.5x37.5-cm) rectangles—one for each child. Cut self-adhesive paper into 12x16-inch (30x40-cm) rectangles—two for each child. Pour paint into shallow containers. Photocopy the Lord's Prayer Pattern onto colored paper—one for each child. Cover work area with newspaper.

Instruct each child in the following procedures:

■ Crumple brown packaging paper rectangle into a small wad, then smooth out carefully. Repeat until paper is as soft as cloth.

■ Cut out Lord's Prayer and glue onto paper rectangle (see sketch).

■ Use paints and printing objects to decorate place mat with safari-theme design. Let dry.

■ Lay one piece of adhesive paper on table, sticky side up. Gently pull off backing.

■ Place paper rectangle on top of adhesive paper and smooth out from center. (Have children work in pairs on this step.)

■ Partially pull off backing of second piece of adhesive. Lay sticky portion on back of place mat and continue peeling as you smooth it out.

■ Trim edges of adhesive paper.

Enrichment Idea: Children letter prayer directly on place mat.

Zungumza: Who can say the Lord's Prayer from memory? (Allow those who know it to recite it together.) **What is your favorite part of the prayer? Jesus taught His disciples how to pray using this prayer as an example.**

Our Father which art in heaven, Hallowed be thy name. Thy kingdom come. Thy will be done in earth, as *it is* in heaven. Give us this day our daily bread. And forgive us our debts, as we forgive our debtors. And lead us not into temptation, but deliver us from evil: For thine is the kingdom, and the power, and the glory, for ever. Amen.
Matthew 6:9-13 (*KJV*)

Paper bag

Clear adhesive-backed paper

Our Father which art in heaven, Hallowed be thy name. Thy kingdom come. Thy will be done in earth, as *it is* in heaven. Give us this day our daily bread. And forgive us our debts, as we forgive our debtors. And lead us not into temptation, but deliver us from evil: For thine is the kingdom, and the power, and the glory, for ever. Amen.

Matthew 6:9-13 (KJV)

Forgiveness Banner

Materials: African Forgiveness Symbol, plain white or light-colored fabric, dark-colored crayons, scratch paper, pencils, permanent felt markers, scissors, measuring stick, newspapers, paper towels, iron. For each child—one 8½x11-inch (21.5x27.5-cm) sheet of coarse sandpaper. *Optional*—sewing machine, 12-inch (30-cm) dowels, yarn.

Preparation: Cut fabric into 10½x13-inch (26.25x32.5-cm) rectangles—one for each child. Copy the Forgiveness Symbol onto scratch paper and post so all children can see it. Cover work area with newspapers. Preheat iron to medium-high setting.

Instruct each child in the following procedures:

■ On scratch paper, and using a pencil, design a banner that uses the Forgiveness Symbol and the words "Forgive each other."

■ Use crayons to draw your design and the forgiveness symbol on sandpaper. (Leave space for the words but do NOT write them on sandpaper or they will be backwards.) Crayon must be applied heavily, or it will not transfer when ironing.

■ When design is completed, lay sandpaper face up on pad of newspapers. Lay fabric over sandpaper and cover fabric with two layers of paper toweling (sketch a).

■ Iron entire area slowly for 10-15 seconds.

■ Peel fabric away from sandpaper.

■ With felt markers, letter "Forgive each other" on banner (sketch b).

Enrichment Idea: Before class, use sewing machine to stitch a casing at top of banner. In class, children slide dowel into casing and tie yarn at each end to form a hanger (sketch b).

Simplification: Print Forgiveness Symbol on sheets of paper to make paper banners.

Zungumza: When is it hard to forgive someone? Sometimes it's easier to hit back or call someone a name than it is to act in a loving way. Just as God forgives us for the hurtful things we do, we can forgive others. The symbol we used on our banners means forgiveness in an African language. It can help us remember to forgive others.

a. Iron — Paper towels — Sandpaper — Fabric — Newspaper

b.

African Forgiveness Symbol

Praying Puppet
(20-30 MINUTES)

Materials: Collar Pattern, light weight cardboard, various colors of construction paper, measuring stick, scissors, pencil, felt pens, glue. For each child—one paper lunch sack, three buttons. *Optional:* Hole punch, paper fasteners, pony beads, yarn, tape.

Preparation: Trace Collar Pattern onto light weight cardboard and cut out one pattern for every four children. Cut out 2-inch (5-cm) squares from construction paper—two for each child. *For optional safari hat:* For each child—on construction paper, trace an 8-inch (20-cm) circle with a 6-inch (15-cm) circle inside. Cut out both circles (sketch e). Cut 1x7-inch (2.5x17.5-cm) construction paper strips—three strips for each child. Cut yarn into 18-inch (45-cm) lengths—one for each child.

Instruct each child in the following procedures:

■ Lay bag flat. Draw eyelashes on bottom of bag (sketch a).

■ Open flap and draw open eyes. Add nose and mouth (sketch b).

■ Trace a collar pattern on construction paper and cut out.

■ To make pockets, fold down one side of each paper square (sketch c).

■ Glue on pockets, collar and buttons (sketch d).

Enrichment Idea: Make safari hat. Children punch holes in the middle of each paper strip. Put paper fastener through holes in the three paper strips as in sketch f. Fold ½ inch (1.25 cm) on ends of strips (sketch f). With adult help, push strips up through circle (brim of hat). Glue or tape tabs to underside of brim. Tape yarn ends to underside of hat. Push pony bead over ends of yarn and tie a knot (sketch g). Glue hat to back of bag.

Zungumza: When we pray, we usually close our eyes. Sometimes we fold our hands. Closing our eyes and folding our hands helps us to be quiet and still. Praying is talking with God. We can talk to Him any time we want because He is always listening to us. When do you like to pray?

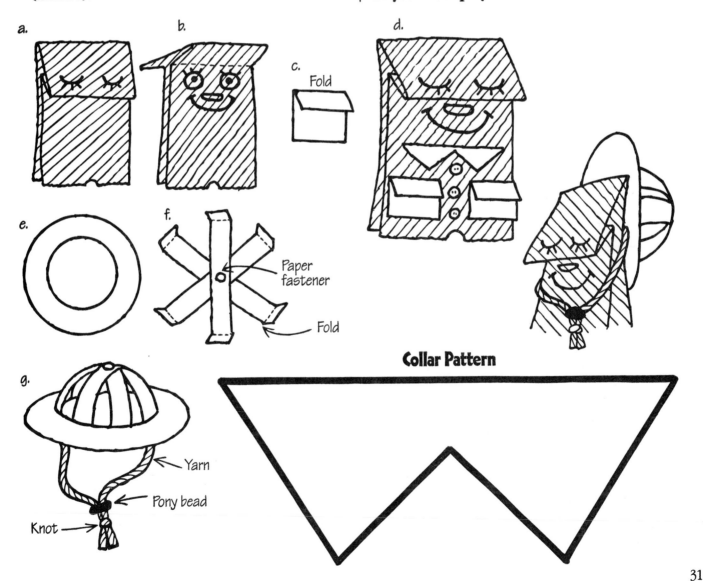

a.
b.
c. Fold
d.
e.
f. Paper fastener Fold
g. Yarn Pony bead Knot

Collar Pattern

31

Paw Print Bookmark

(20-30 MINUTES)

Materials: Paw Print Patterns, lightweight cardboard, card stock, felt, ruler, yarn, scissors, felt pens, pencils, glue.

Preparation: Trace paw print patterns onto cardboard to make one of each pattern for every two to three children. Cut yarn into 10-inch (25-cm) lengths—one for each child.

Instruct each child in the following procedures:

- Choose one pattern and trace onto card stock four times. Cut out.
- Cut shapes from felt for claws, toenails, pads, etc. and glue onto two of the prints (see sketch).
- Letter "Lead us not" on third print and "into temptation" on fourth print.

- Spread glue on backs of two lettered prints.
- Place one end of yarn on each glued print.
- Press two decorated prints onto the two glued prints, sealing in yarn.

Zungumza: In the Bible, Jesus taught us to pray, "Lead us not into temptation," because He knows that God helps us stay away from trouble if we ask Him. Reading the Bible helps us know what to do when we are tempted to do wrong. You can use your Paw Print Bookmark in your Bible. It will remind you that God leads you *away* from trouble, when you pray for His help.

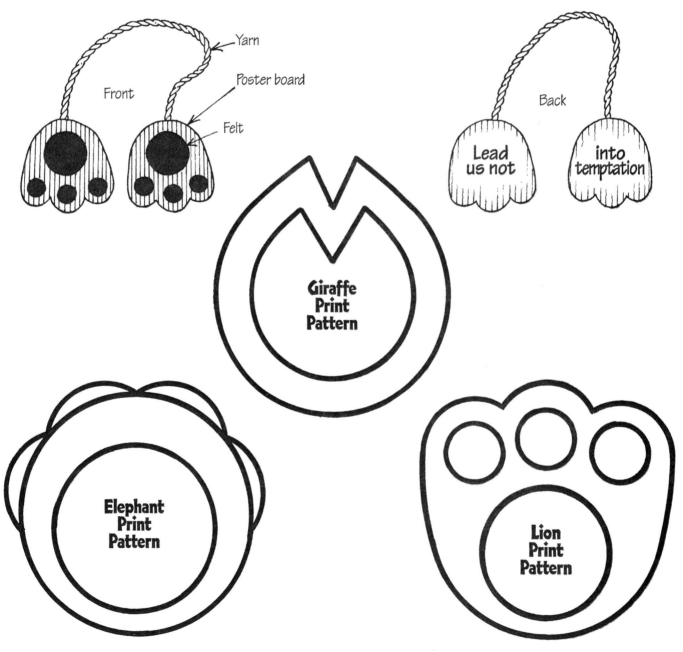

Scenic Prayer Journal
(20-25 MINUTES)

▼▲

Materials: White poster board, tissue paper in a variety of colors, paintbrushes, shallow containers, water, glue, craft knife, scissors, hole punch, ruler, sheets of plain white paper, newspaper. For each child—two paper fasteners.

Preparation: Cut some of the poster board into 9x13-inch (22.5x32.5-cm) rectangles—one for each child. Use craft knife to score two lines on each piece of poster board as shown in sketch a. Use a hole punch to punch two holes in poster board as shown in sketch a. Punch two holes at the top of sheets of paper (the same distance apart as holes in poster board). Cut remaining poster board into 9x12-inch (22.5x30-cm) rectangles—one for each child. Dilute glue with a small amount of water in containers. Cover work area with newspaper.

Instruct each child in the following procedures:

■ Tear tissue paper into different size pieces.

■ Brush glue mixture onto smaller poster board piece.

■ Place torn tissue paper onto sticky surface, one piece at a time, to create an African scene (sketch b). Include sun, grass, hills, river or lake and trees.

■ Brush more glue over torn tissue paper. Allow to dry.

■ Fold larger poster board piece along score lines.

■ Glue top edge of small poster board onto front flap of larger poster board (sketch c).

■ Insert paper fasteners into holes to secure paper inside journal (sketch d).

Zungumza: In your prayer journal you can write your prayers and the names of people you want to pray for or you can draw a picture of something you want to pray about. God wants us to spend time with Him in prayer. He listens to us when we pray out loud. He hears the prayers we think silently. He even knows the prayers we write to Him. God always listens!

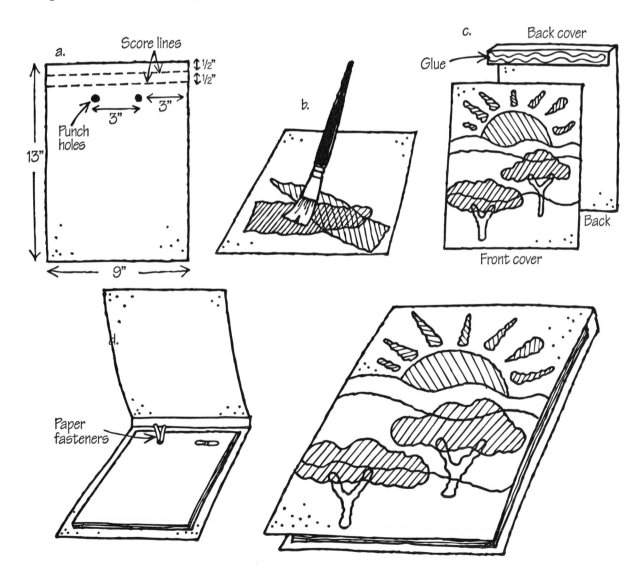

Wooden Xylophone

(20-25 MINUTES)

Materials: Acrylic paint in a variety of colors, paintbrushes, shallow containers, 1 ½-inch (3.75-cm) wide hard wood strips ¼-inch (.625-cm) thick, ⅜-inch (1.875-cm) dowels, saw, craft glue, packaging tape, scissors, pencil, ruler, newspaper. For each child—one adult-size shoe box, one medium-size wood bead with ⅜-inch (1.875-cm) hole, one clothespin.

Preparation: Saw hardwood strips into the following sizes, one of each for each child: 6½ inches (16.25 cm), 6 inches (15 cm), 5½ inches (13.75 cm), 5 inches (12.5 cm), 4½ inches (11.25 cm), 4 inches (10 cm), 3½ inches (8.75 cm). Cut dowels into 12-inch (30-cm) lengths. Cut a triangular piece out of bottom of each shoe box (sketch a). Cover work area with newspaper. Pour paint into shallow containers.

Instruct each child in the following procedures:

■ Fold in the cut corners of shoe box so corners overlap. Secure side piece to bottom of box with a piece of packaging tape (sketch b).

■ Glue cut sides together and secure with clothespin until glue sets (sketch b).

■ Paint shoe box and wood strips in various colors and designs. Let dry.

■ Glue end of dowel into wood bead to make mallet.

■ Glue wood pieces onto top of box, allowing space between each piece (sketch c).

■ When glue has dried, children play xylophones by striking wood strips with the mallet.

Zungumza: In some African villages, people use many types of materials to make instruments. Drums are made from gourds; hollow sticks are filled with small pebbles or seeds to shake; other instruments, similar to your xylophone, are made from wood. When people in African churches praise God they sometimes use instruments to make music. We can use rhythm and music to tell God how happy we are that He is our loving Father in heaven. This is a way of praising God.

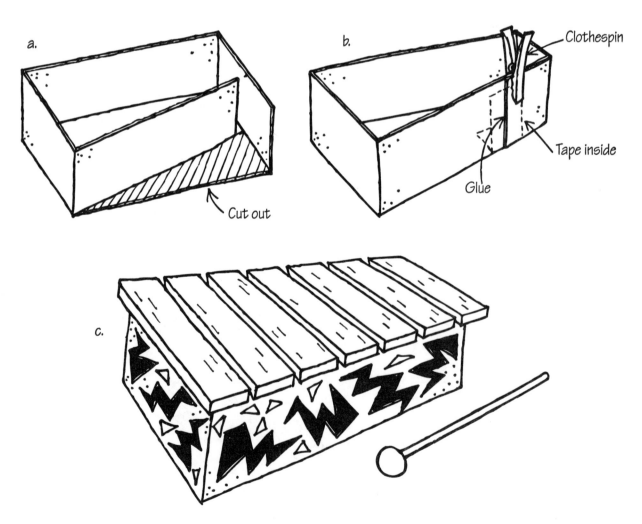

a.

Cut out

b.

Clothespin

Tape inside

Glue

c.

African Trinket Box
(20-25 MINUTES)

Materials: Fabric in a variety of bright colors and patterns, construction paper, scissors, glue, ruler, pencil, paintbrushes, shallow containers. For each child—one round ice cream carton with lid.

Preparation: Cut ice cream cartons down to a 2½-inch (6.25-cm) height (sketch a). Cut fabric into 3x4-inch (7.5x10-cm) pieces. Using the ice cream lid as a pattern, trace and cut fabric into circles ¼ inch (.625 cm) smaller than the size of the lid—two for each child. Cut construction paper into 16x2¼-inch (40x5.625-cm) strips—one for each child. Pour glue into shallow containers.

Instruct each child in the following procedures:

■ Brush glue on outside of carton and smooth fabric strips over glue.

■ Glue fabric ends over top edge of carton to the inside and over bottom edge (sketch b), covering carton completely with fabric.

■ Glue one fabric circle to the bottom outside of carton, covering fabric strip ends (sketch c).

■ Glue the other fabric circle to the top of carton lid (sketch c).

■ Glue construction paper strip to the inside of box (sketch d).

■ When glue is dry, put lid on box.

Enrichment Idea: Glue felt circle to inside bottom of box.

Zungumza: Many African children like to wear clothes made from bright colored fabric, like the fabric you glued on your boxes. What is your favorite color, (Tony)? What is something God has made that is (yellow)?

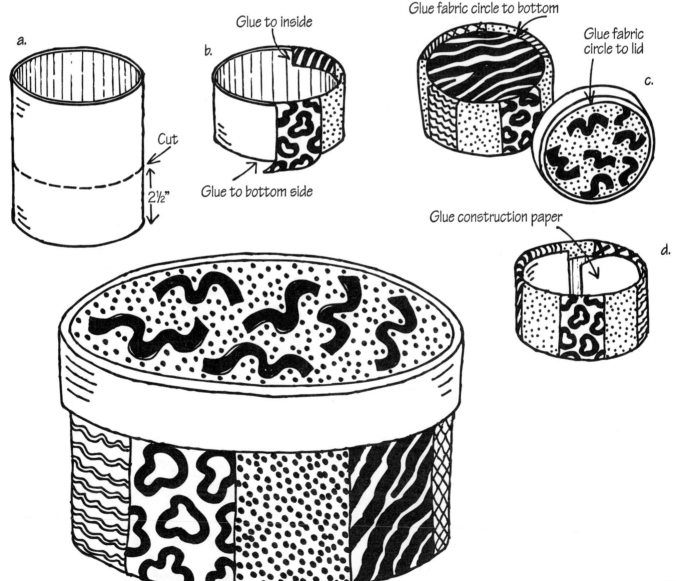

a.

Cut

2½"

b.

Glue to inside

Glue to bottom side

Glue fabric circle to bottom

Glue fabric circle to lid

c.

Glue construction paper

d.

Heavy Hippo Doorstop
(35-40 MINUTES)

Materials: Eye and Ear Patterns, acrylic paints in grey, blue and white, blue glitter fabric paint with fine tip, card stock, sand, paper cups, paintbrushes, shallow containers, black permanent felt pens, glue, self-adhesive paper hole reinforcements, pencil, scissors, ruler, photocopier, newspaper. For each child—one half-gallon milk carton, two 20-mm wiggle eyes, one tongue depressor.

Preparation: Cut milk cartons in half—one for each child. Photocopy Eye and Ear Patterns onto card stock. Cut tongue depressors 1 inch (2.5 cm) from each end. Discard middle piece of tongue depressor. Cover work area with newspaper. Pour acrylic paint into shallow containers.

Instruct each child in the following procedures:

■ Use paper cup to pour sand into bottom portion of milk carton.

■ Spread glue around bottom portion of milk carton (sketch a). Place top portion of milk carton over bottom portion.

■ Glue top opening of milk carton together.

■ Cut out card stock eye pattern and ears and glue onto top of milk carton (sketch b).

■ Paint top half of milk carton and card stock eyes and ears grey.

■ Paint bottom half of carton blue (sketch c). Let dry.

■ Paint tongue depressor pieces white to make tusks.

■ With black felt pen, draw a line around the middle of the grey portion of carton to make mouth (sketch c).

■ Stick hole reinforcements onto top edge of carton for nostrils (sketch c).

■ Glue on wiggle eyes and tusks.

■ Use fabric paint to make waves in the water.

Zungumza: A hippo is so heavy it will sink to the bottom of a lake. It can hold its breath for a long time while it runs underwater, looking for fish and plants to eat. The hippo you made is very heavy too. You can use it as a doorstop to keep a door open or as a bookend to hold your books on a shelf.

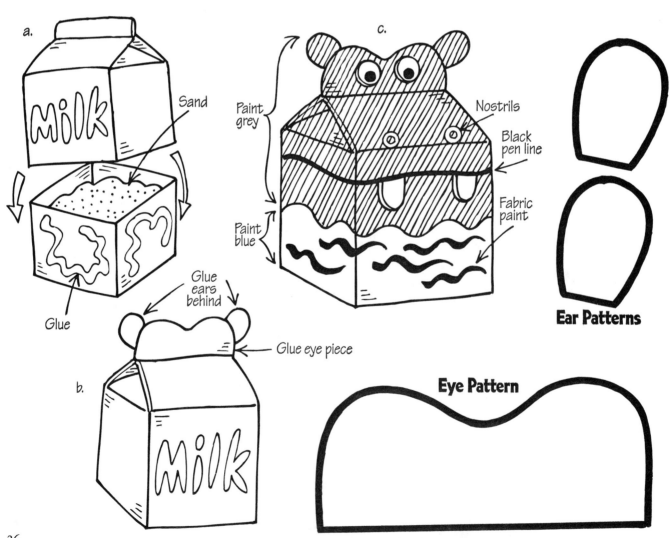

Ear Patterns

Eye Pattern

Giraffe Tape Measure
(20-25 MINUTES)

Materials: Giraffe Head Pattern, yellow poster board, yellow and brown liquid tempera paint, paintbrushes, used sponges, clothespins, brown felt pens, pencil, masking tape, craft glue, scissors, shallow containers, newspaper. For each child—one bath soap box (flaps intact), yellow dressmaker measuring tape, one bendable drinking straw.

Preparation: Trace Giraffe Head Pattern onto yellow poster board and cut out—two for each child. Use tip of scissors to poke a hole in both sides of each box (sketch a). Make holes large enough to fit a drinking straw. Trim drinking straws to about 5 inches (12.5 cm). Cut a slit in the side of each box near the opening (sketch a). Cut sponges into several small geometric shapes. Clip clothespins onto sponge cutouts for easier handling. Cover work area with newspaper. Pour paint into shallow containers.

Instruct each child in the following procedures:
■ Paint soap box yellow. Allow paint to dry.
■ Insert straw through holes in box and bend the end (sketch b).

■ With teacher's help, tape end of measuring tape to the straw inside box (sketch b).
■ Thread opposite end of measuring tape through slit in top of box (sketch b).
■ Wind the rest of measuring tape around straw by turning straw from outside the box.
■ Glue giraffe heads onto both sides of measuring tape at the ½-inch (1.25-cm) mark (sketch c). Hold while glue dries. Glue box flaps closed.
■ Dip sponge into brown paint and make giraffe markings on the box (sketch d).
■ Use felt pen to draw eyes, nose and mane on both sides of giraffe's head (sketch d).

Zungumza: **Giraffes in Africa are so tall they have a hard time bending down to drink at the watering hole. But they can reach the leaves of tall trees that other animals can't reach. They get the water they need from the moisture in the leaves. God provides just what every animal needs in the hot African wilderness. He provides what we need too.**

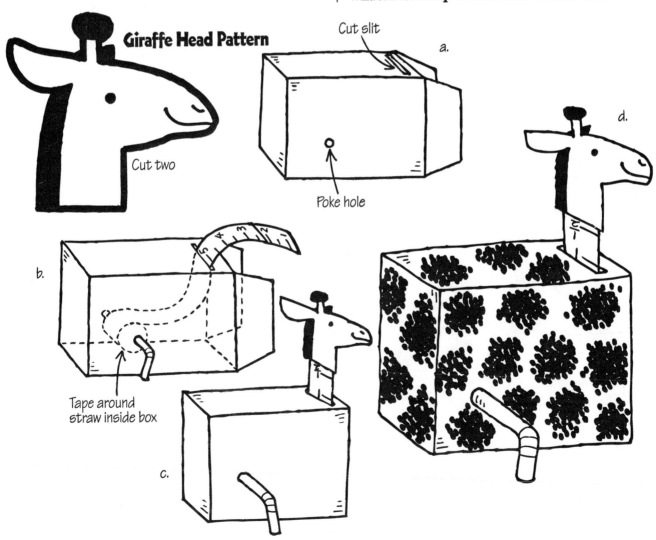

Giraffe Head Pattern

Cut two

Cut slit

a.

Poke hole

d.

b.

Tape around straw inside box

c.

Stand-Up Safari Animals

Materials: Animal Patterns, card stock in several bright colors, yarn, chenille wire, small wiggle eyes, felt pens, hole punch, craft glue, scissors, pencils.

Preparation: Trace Animal Patterns onto card stock to make several patterns of each. Cut out. Cut remaining card stock into 4x6-inch (10x15-cm) pieces.

Instruct each child in the following procedures:

■ Fold a card stock piece in half and lay an Animal Body Pattern on fold (sketch a). Trace around pattern. Cut out.

■ Choosing appropriate patterns, trace and cut out animal heads and ears using card stock pieces.

■ Glue wiggle eyes on faces.

■ Decorate faces with felt pens, yarn, chenille wire, or cut-out card stock.

■ Decorate animal bodies.

■ For elephant, hippo, lion or cheetah—cut and fold back tabs on body (sketch b).

■ Glue heads to bodies (sketch c).

Decorating Animals:

■ Zebra: Glue on black chenille wire or yarn for stripes, mane and tail.

■ Giraffe: Cut out irregular small card stock shapes for giraffe markings and glue on. Glue on brown yarn to make short mane and tail. Use chenille wire for giraffe antlers.

■ Lion: Glue face in the middle of mane. Glue chenille wire or yarn on mane. Glue on yarn for tail.

■ Cheetah: With hole punch, punch out card stock spots and glue on. Glue on tail.

■ Hippo: Cut out small ears and tusks. Glue on.

■ Elephants: Glue ears on back of head. Cut a strip of card stock and fold accordion-style to make trunk. Cut out white tusks. Glue trunk and tusks on face.

■ Add nostrils, mouths, hooves, etc. with felt pens.

Enrichment Idea: Children assemble several animals, punch holes in bodies and tie fishing line through holes to make mobiles (See Sunshine Mobile on page 20 or Reminder Chimes on page 53 for mobile construction ideas.)

Zungumza: What makes a (zebra) different from every other animal, (Alicia)? God created all the animals and He made them each a little different. He created people and made each of us different, too. How are you different from your friends? How are you the same?

a. Fold

b. Cut

Fold

c. Glue

38

Stand-Up Safari Animal Patterns

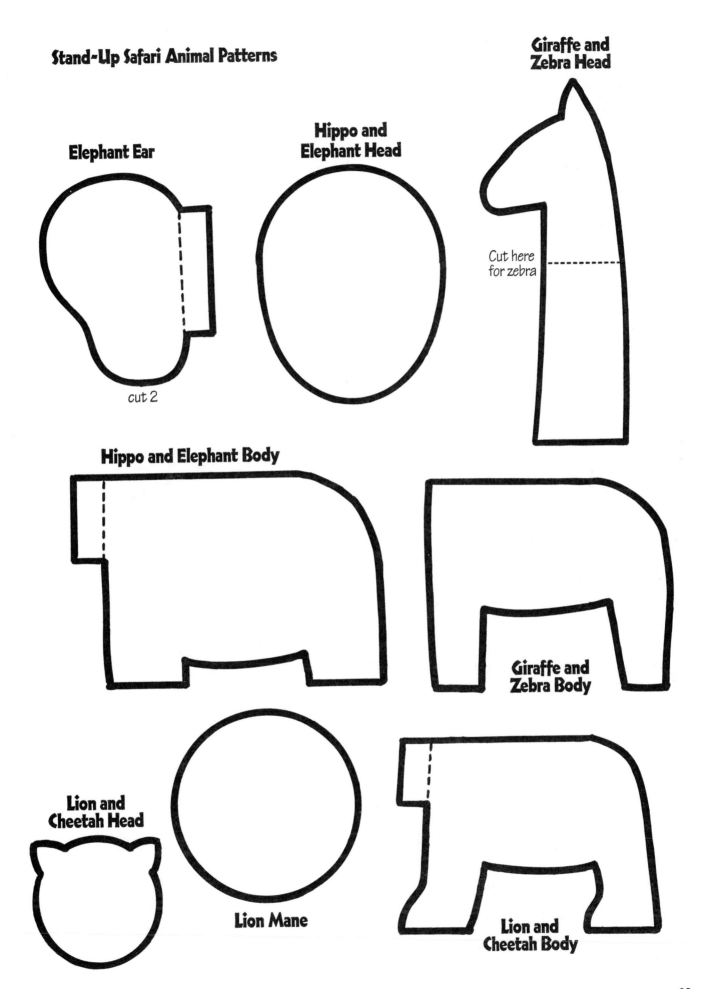

Elephant Ear

cut 2

Hippo and
Elephant Head

Giraffe and
Zebra Head

Cut here
for zebra

Hippo and Elephant Body

Giraffe and
Zebra Body

Lion and
Cheetah Head

Lion Mane

Lion and
Cheetah Body

Decorated Ostrich Eggs
(TWO-DAY CRAFT/25-30 MINUTES)

Materials: Newspapers, tempera paint in a variety of colors, paintbrushes, flour, measuring cup, water, shallow containers, string, clear acrylic spray, scissors, ruler. For each child—one medium-size pear- or egg-shaped balloon, one disposable cup.

Preparation: DAY ONE: Mix one part flour to one part water in containers. Cover work area with newspapers. Cut newspaper into ½-inch (1.25-cm) strips. Cut string into 1-yard (90-cm) lengths—one for each child. **DAY TWO:** Pour paint into shallow containers. Cover work area with newspapers.

Instruct each child in the following procedures:
DAY ONE:

■ Inflate balloon to a medium size and knot. Tie string to balloon knot.

■ Tear paper strips into approximately 6-inch (15-cm) lengths. Dip paper strips into flour mixture and cover entire balloon, leaving string free (sketch a). Allow ostrich egg to dry one or two days.

DAY TWO:

■ Stand ostrich egg on disposable cup to paint.

■ Paint a variety of colors and African designs (sketch b). Allow to dry.

■ Spray egg with clear acrylic spray outdoors.

■ Use string to hang decorated ostrich egg in your room.

Enrichment Idea: Make several eggs in graduated sizes and attach together to hang in a row.

Zungumza: An ostrich is a huge type of bird that lives in Africa. One ostrich egg weighs as much as 24 chicken eggs and is about the same size as a cantaloupe. An ostrich eggshell is so thick that a man can only open it with a saw or a hammer! A baby ostrich's beak must be very strong and sharp to be able to break out of its shell.

a.

b.

Zebra Wind Twirler
(35-40 MINUTES)

Materials: Clear acrylic spray, black and white tempera paints, thick craft glue, black yarn, measuring stick, scissors, paintbrushes, shallow containers, newspapers, glue gun, glue sticks. For each child—20 tongue depressors, five spring-type clothespins.

Preparation: Cover work area with newspapers. Pour paint into containers. Cut yarn into 5-foot (1.5-m) lengths—one for each child. Plug in glue gun.

Instruct each child in the following procedures:
■ Paint 10 tongue depressors white, front and back.
■ Paint 10 tongue depressors black, front and back.
■ When sticks are dry, place one black stick on table and glue (with craft glue) one white stick on top of it, forming a narrow *X* (sketch a).
■ Alternating black and white, glue two more sticks on top of the first two sticks. Clip a clothespin to the center of glued sticks to hold them together while glue dries (sketch b).
■ Beginning with a black stick, glue four more sticks together and clip with a clothespin. Continue making four-stick sections until only four sticks remain.

■ Glue three of the remaining sticks together.
■ Glue the middle of the yarn length to the center of the top stick. Glue the last stick on top of the yarn (sketch c). Knot yarn ends together.
■ With teacher's help, use glue gun to glue all five sections of twirler together in a continuous spiral (sketch d).
■ In outdoor area, spray with acrylic spray.

Enrichment Idea: Children knot yarn a few inches above completed twirler and string pony beads on both yarn ends before knotting ends together near top. Children can add more sticks to twirler if time permits. Additional sticks can be added throughout the week. The more sticks used, the greater the spiral effect.

Zungumza: Why do you think zebras have stripes? Zebras have stripes to help them hide from animals that hunt them. In Africa it's hard to see a zebra in the shadows or in the tall grass. A zebra's stripes help to protect it. God protects us from getting hurt, too. He gave us families to take care of us. We can pray and ask God to protect us when we are worried or afraid.

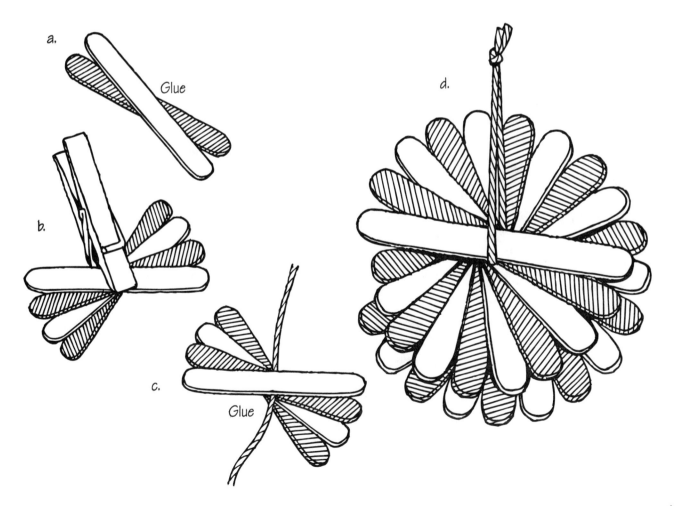

a.

Glue

b.

c.

Glue

d.

African Animal Frame
(25-30 MINUTES)

Materials: Picture Frame Pattern, poster board, green, yellow, brown and blue tissue paper, green twisted paper (available at craft stores), safari animal crackers, tempera paints, paintbrushes, shallow containers, scissors, glue, ruler, newspapers, water.

Preparation: Cut tissue paper into 2-inch (5-cm) wide strips. Use pattern to cut out one poster board frame and one poster board frame backing for each child. Cut twisted paper into 12-inch (30-cm) lengths—one for each child. Cover work area with newspapers. Pour glue into containers and dilute with a little water. Pour paint into containers.

Instruct each child in the following procedures:
- Choose two or three animal crackers and paint with tempera paint. Set aside to dry.
- Tear tissue paper strips into squares. Brush picture frame with glue and cover with tissue paper, overlapping squares. You may use only one color of tissue, or make a landscape using green, brown or yellow for land and blue for sky (sketch a).
- Brush a layer of glue over tissue, folding tissue onto back of frame along edges.

- Untwist green twisted paper length.
- Cut off 1 to 2 inches (2.5 to 5 cm) of paper and glue on bottom of frame as tall "grass."
- Glue painted animal crackers in and behind "grass" (sketch b).
- Brush animal crackers and paper grass with glue to seal.
- For hanger, glue the ends of the remaining twisted paper length to the frame backing (sketch c).
- Glue the frame back to the decorated frame. Glue only along the bottom edge and sides to allow for picture insertion at top (sketch c).

Zungumza: It's important to listen and follow instructions when you make your picture frame. (Donovan), what would happen if you didn't follow the instructions or listen to the teacher? (I wouldn't know how to do the craft.) **God gave us instructions to follow, too. They are in the Bible. The Bible tells us how to treat other people and how to love God. The Bible helps us learn what is right. We can pray to God and ask Him to help us follow His instructions.**

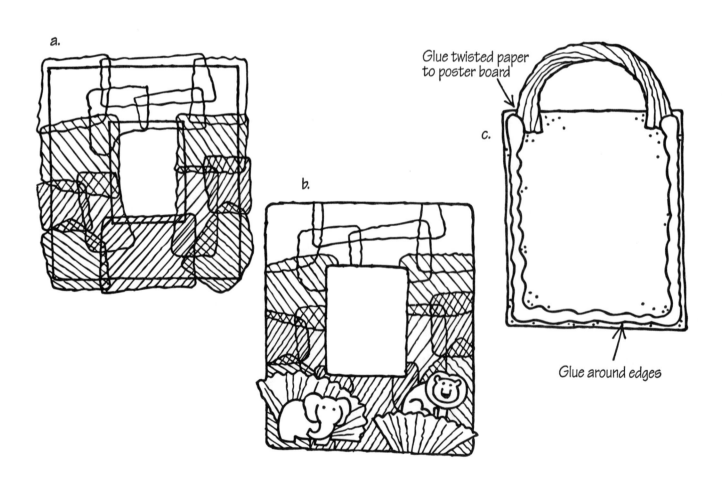

a.

b.

c.

Glue twisted paper to poster board

Glue around edges

African Animal Frame Pattern

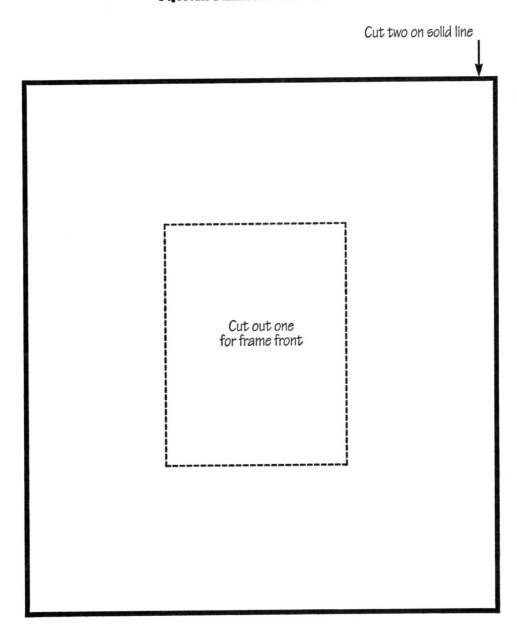

Cut two on solid line

Cut out one
for frame front

Daily Bread Basket
(20-30 MINUTES)

▼▲▼▲▼▲▼▲▼▲▼▲▼▲▼▲▼▲▼▲▼▲▼▲▼▲▼▲▼▲▼▲▼▲▼▲▼▲

Materials: Basket Pattern, brightly colored poster board, construction paper, raffia, pencil, felt pens, ruler, scissors, glue, spring-type clothespins.

Preparation: Using pattern, cut one poster board basket for each child. With point of scissors, score along dotted lines (sketch a) and bend flaps up to make sides of basket. Cut raffia in 3-foot (90-cm) lengths—several for each child. Cut construction paper into 1x3-inch (2.5x7.5-cm) strips— five for each child.

Instruct each child in the following procedures:

■ Letter "Our Daily Bread" in center of basket.

■ Glue end of raffia length inside basket (sketch b). Weave raffia around the inside of one flap of basket and outside the next (sketch b). When one raffia length is completed, glue the end to the poster board and glue on a new raffia length. Continue weaving until raffia is ½-inch (1.25-cm) from top of basket. Cut raffia and fasten end with glue.

■ Finish off top of basket by gluing on folded strips of construction paper (sketch c).

■ Use clothespins to hold paper in place as glue dries (sketch c).

Simplification Idea: Use thick craft yarn or rug yarn instead of raffia.

Zungumza: **What kinds of things can this basket hold? What things does God give us that can't be held in a basket? Your Daily Bread Basket can remind you to thank God for everything He gives us.**

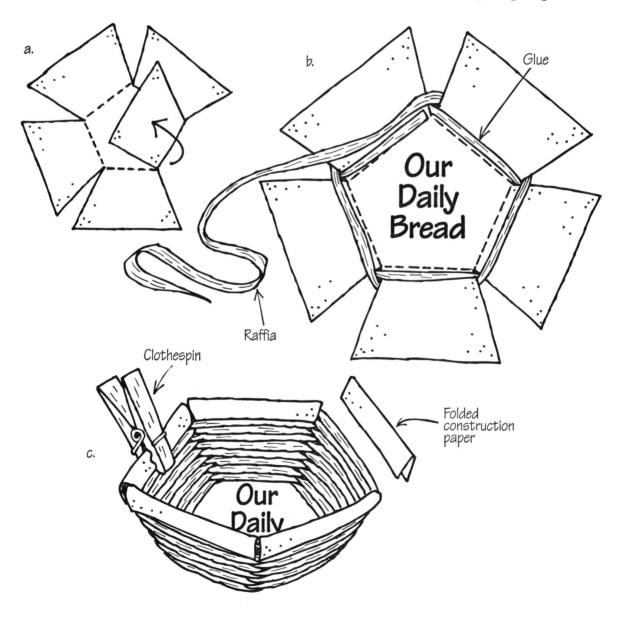

Daily Bread Basket Pattern

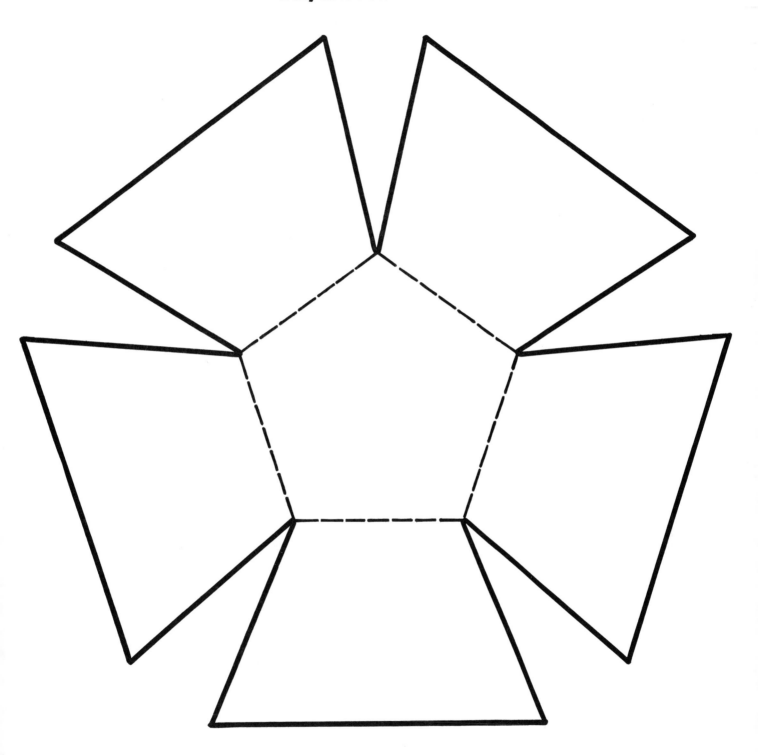

Pom-Pom Lion
(15-20 MINUTES)

Materials: Brown bump chenille wire, yellow chenille wire, ruler, scissors, craft glue. For each child—two 1-inch (2.5-cm) yellow pom-poms, five ½-inch (1.25-cm) yellow pom-poms, two ¼-inch (.625-cm) yellow pom-poms, one 1-inch (2.5-cm) yellow tinsel pom-pom, one ⅛-inch (.3125-cm) brown pom-pom, two small wiggle eyes.

Preparation: Cut bumps in brown chenille wire apart— one bump for each child. Cut yellow chenille wire into 3-inch (7.5-cm) pieces—one piece for each child.

Instruct each child in the following procedures:

■ Glue two large pom-poms together to make lion body.

■ Glue four medium-size pom-poms to body to make feet.

■ Make tail by bending one end of yellow chenille wire around the middle of the brown chenille bump (sketch a). Twist chenille bump ends together. Glue tail to lion body.

■ On tinsel pom-pom, glue two small yellow pom-poms to make ears. Glue on wiggle eyes. Below eyes, glue medium-size yellow pom-pom. Glue on brown pom-pom to make nose.

■ Glue head on lion body. Allow glue to dry.

Zungumza: Most wild cats like to be alone or in pairs, but lions live in groups called "prides." Lions share their food with each other. A mother lion will baby-sit other lioness' cubs when they go hunting. Lions watch out for each other. How do your friends and family watch out for each other? Help each other?

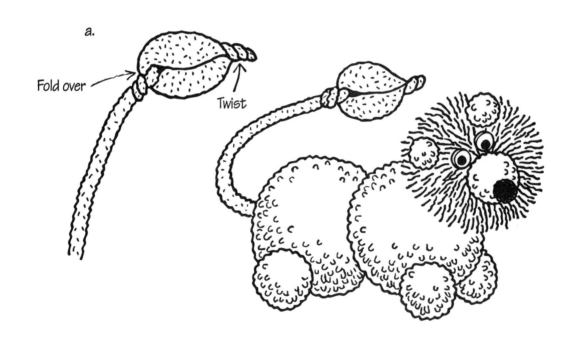

a.

Fold over

Twist

Section Three/Grades 4-6

Crafts for Older Elementary

Trying to plan craft projects for older children has driven many teachers prematurely grey. The challenge is that while these children have well-developed skills to complete projects, they also have well-developed preferences about what they want to do. Thus a project that may challenge their abilities may be scorned because it somehow is not appealing to these young sophisticates. Then the next project will seem too juvenile to the adult, but will click with the kids!

There's no justice! And a sense of humor surely helps. One helpful device is to filter a craft idea through a panel of experts—two or three fifth graders. If they like it, chances are the rest of the group will, also. Then, the better you get to know your particular students, the better your batting average will be.

We think you'll find projects in this section to satisfy the varied tastes of older elementary children!

Safari Clipboard

(25-30 MINUTES)

Materials: Heavy cardboard, craft knife, prepasted wallpaper or self-adhesive paper (in African-type design), scissors, ruler, small containers of water, sponges, newspapers. For each child—one metal spring clip (purchase from stationery stores).

Preparation: Use craft knife to cut cardboard into 9x12-inch (22.5x30-cm) rectangles—one for each child. Cut wallpaper into 15x20-inch (37.5x50-cm) rectangles—one for each child. Cover work area with newspapers. Place containers of water and sponges on work area.

Instruct each child in the following procedures:

■ Place wallpaper facedown. Place cardboard on top of wallpaper. Cut excess paper off each corner (sketch a).

■ Remove cardboard from wallpaper. Use sponge dipped in water to wet back of wallpaper rectangle.

■ Wrap cardboard with wallpaper (sketch b).

■ Using wet sponge, smooth wrinkles out of wallpaper. Let dry.

■ Clip the spring clip to top of clipboard (sketch c).

Enrichment Ideas: Provide scissors and ruler. Allow children to measure and cut their own pieces of wallpaper. Provide paper for children to clip to their clipboards.

Zungumza: Safari means "journey" in Swahili. Often people who go on safari keep a record of what they see and do on their journeys. You can use your clipboard to write down what you do on your family vacation. You can also use it to keep a daily record of your prayers to God.

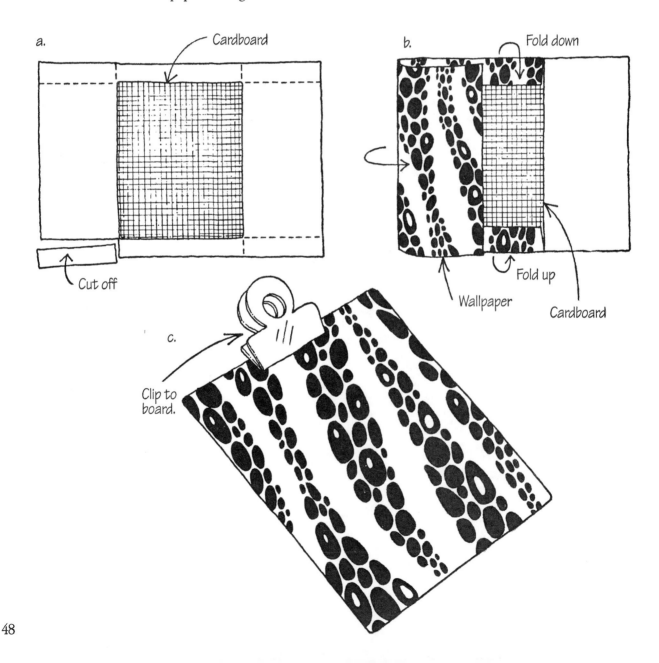

a. Cardboard / Cut off

b. Fold down / Fold up / Wallpaper / Cardboard

c. Clip to board.

African Cloth
(35-40 MINUTES)

Materials: White fabric sheet torn into 24x24-inch (60x60-cm) squares, one large foil roasting pan and one Crock-Pot for every four to five children, kitchen knife, one or two irons, paper towels, newspapers, fabric dye, soap and water or disposable baby wipes for clean-up. For every two children—one white candle (taper).

Preparation: Cut candles in half. Cover all work surfaces with a thick layer of newspapers. In roasting pans, mix fabric dye according to package instructions. Allow dye to cool to room temperature. Pour 3 inches (7.5 cm) of water into each Crock-Pot and turn temperature to high. Turn temperature of Crock-Pots to low when children arrive. In an area away from work surfaces, heat dry irons to medium heat.

Instruct each child in the following procedures:

■ Lay fabric flat on a pad of newspapers.

■ Dip end of candle 1 inch (2.5 cm) in hot water in Crock-Pot until wax is very soft (sketch a).

■ Draw a design with softened end of candle on fabric, dipping candle in water as needed to re-soften wax. Make sure wax is applied heavily to fabric (sketch b).

■ Immerse waxed fabric in dye and let it soak for 15-20 seconds (sketch c).

■ Place four paper towels on top of a pad of newspapers.

■ Remove fabric from dye, carefully wring out excess moisture and lay fabric flat on top of paper towels.

■ Cover fabric with four more paper towels and one layer of newspaper. Carry all layers to ironing area.

■ With teacher's help, iron layer of towels and newspaper until fabric is dry. Heat from the iron will cause wax to soften and be absorbed from the fabric into the paper towels (sketch d).

■ Clean hands using soap and water or baby wipes.

■ Children can wear cloth as a scarf on their head, as many African children do, or around their neck as a safari scarf.

Enrichment Idea: For more finished cloth, teacher hems fabric squares or children may use cloth to cover the "Pocket Passport" or "Jambo Journal."

Zungumza: On holidays, some African men and women wear clothing made out of brightly colored cloth printed with bold patterns. The women wrap long strips of cloth called *kankas* around their bodies and the men wear loose shirts called *dashikis*. Clothing is something we all need, no matter where we live in the world. In the Bible, Jesus says that God clothes even the flowers in the fields (see Matthew 6:28-30) **so He certainly will take care of us and provide for our needs!**

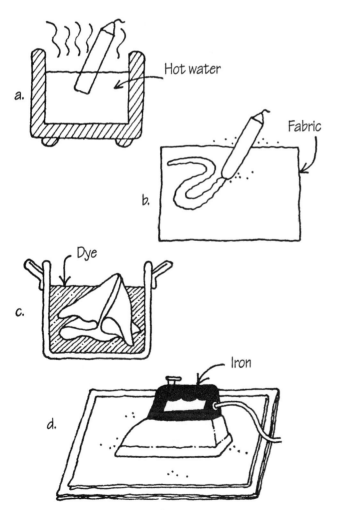

Pocket Passport
(30-40 MINUTES)

▼▲▼▲▼▲▼▲▼▲▼▲▼▲▼▲▼▲▼▲▼▲▼▲▼▲▼▲▼▲▼▲▼

Materials: Passport Patterns 1 and 2, pencil, wing-style billfold inserts (for photos and credit cards), African-print cotton fabric, glue, scissors, poster board, fine tip felt pens, yarn. For each child—four 3x5-inch (7.5x12.5-cm) lined index cards.

Preparation: Trace patterns onto poster board and cut out. Make a set of patterns for every three to four children. Cut fabric into 9x12-inch (22.5x30-cm) pieces—one for each child. Cut index cards in half, eight halves for each child. Remove clip from around billfold inserts so sections can be separated. You will need two sections (four pockets) for each child. Cut yarn into 18-inch (45-cm) lengths.

Instruct each child in the following procedures:

■ Trace Pattern 1 onto fabric one time and cut out.

■ Trace Pattern 2 onto poster board two times and onto fabric two times. Cut out.

■ Thinly coat one side of each poster board piece with glue. Place on wrong side of larger piece of fabric that was cut from Pattern 1 (sketch a).

■ Draw a line of glue around the three outside edges of poster board pieces (sketch b).

■ Fold down each corner of fabric and press onto line of glue. Then fold down edges of fabric over glue and press in place (sketch c).

■ Thinly coat exposed poster board pieces with glue.

■ Place one small fabric piece onto each poster board piece coated with glue and press in place (sketch d). Let dry.

■ On one card draw a picture of yourself and write your name, age and one thing you are thankful for (sketch e).

■ Open billfold insert to center and rest inside book cover so that the center of the insert lines up with the center of the cover. Use yarn to tie insert to cover (sketch f).

■ If time permits, children letter memory verse for each day on five separate cards. Use the additional cards for other drawing or writing.

■ Slide cards into the pockets of billfold insert.

Enrichment Ideas: Children may bring small photos of themselves to glue on index card inserted in the passport. Children earn stickers for attendance or reciting Bible verses and then place stickers on cards in passport.

Zungumza: **What is a passport?** (Students respond.) **When you travel to another country you must always have your passport with you. Officials in that country place a stamp of permission on the passport before allowing you to enter their country. God gives each of us permission to be in His kingdom—His family. Jesus is the passport into God's kingdom. When Jesus died to forgive our sins, and rose again, He made it possible for us to live in God's kingdom. God gives us His stamp of permission when we believe in His Son, Jesus.**

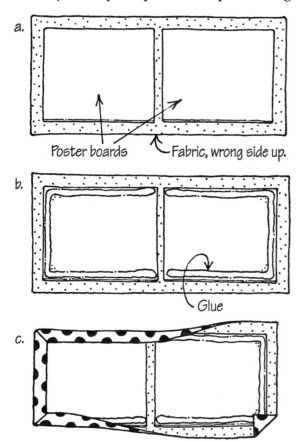

a. Poster boards — Fabric, wrong side up.

b. Glue

c.

e.
Name: Sarah
Age: 9 years old
I'm thankful for:
My mom and dad.

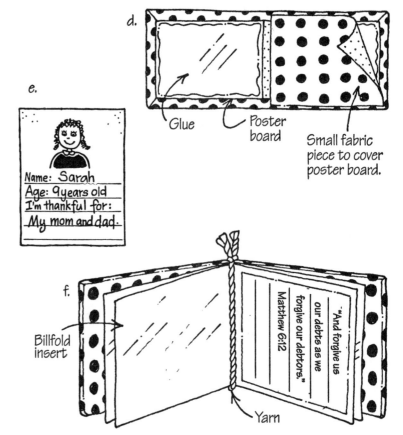

d. Glue — Poster board — Small fabric piece to cover poster board.

f. Billfold insert — "And forgive us our debts as we forgive our debtors." Matthew 6:12 — Yarn

Pocket Passport Patterns

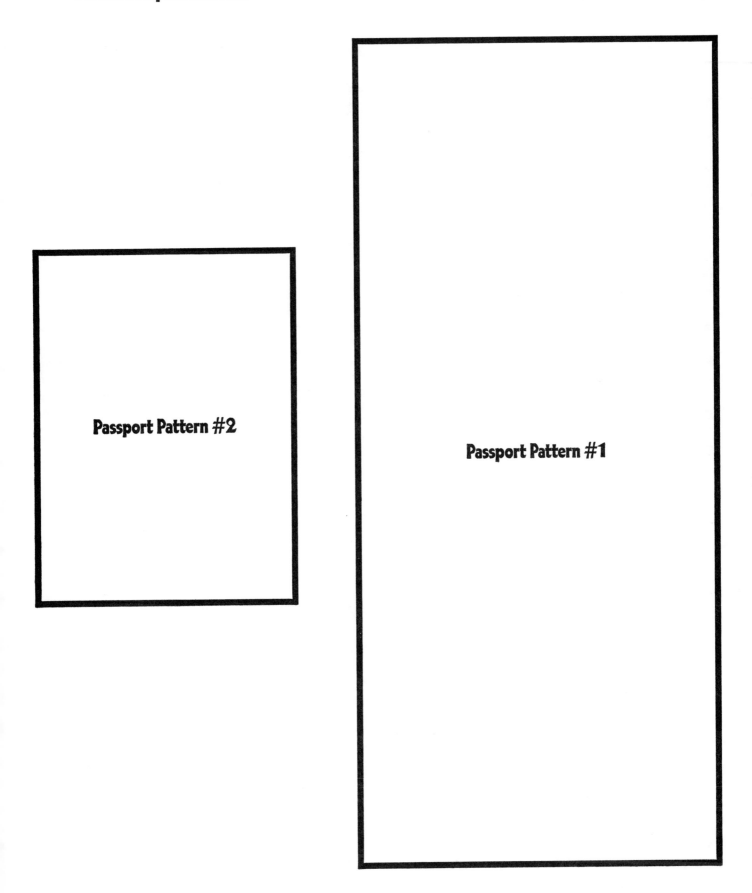

Passport Pattern #2

Passport Pattern #1

Praise Medallion
(35-40 MINUTES)

▼▲▼▲▼▲▼▲▼▲▼▲▼▲▼▲▼▲▼▲▼▲▼▲▼▲▼▲▼▲▼▲▼

Materials: Yarn in various colors, felt, lightweight cardboard, fine-tip felt pens, construction paper, rubber bands, craft glue, scissors, measuring stick, paper cups, paintbrushes, newspapers or newsprint.

Preparation: Cut yarn into 3-foot (.9-m) lengths—6 or 7 for each student. Cut additional yarn into approximately 5-inch (12.5-cm) lengths—four for each student. Cut additional yarn into 2-foot (60-cm) lengths—one for each child. Cut cardboard into 3x5-inch (7.5x12.5-cm) rectangles and 6-inch (15-cm) circles—one rectangle and one circle for each student. Pour glue into paper cups. Cover work area with newspapers.

Instruct each child in the following procedures:

■ Use the cardboard circle as a pattern and with a felt pen draw a circle on the felt. Cut out felt circle.

■ Use brush to paint a thick layer of glue on the cardboard circle.

■ Coil a longer length of yarn on the circle of glue (sketch a). Press yarn into glue as you wind. Continue using other colors of yarn to complete coil. Let dry.

■ Wrap one of the longer lengths of yarn around the rectangular piece of cardboard (sketch b).

■ At top of cardboard, tie yarn together with a shorter piece of yarn (sketch c). Cut through the yarn at the other end and remove yarn from cardboard.

■ To form tassel, wrap a rubber band near tied end of yarn. Cut a small rectangle of felt 2x3 inches (5x7.5 cm) and tightly wrap it on top of rubber band (sketch d). Secure with glue. Repeat this procedure to make three more tassels.

■ Using the 2-foot (60-cm) length of yarn, tie the four tassels near center of yarn (sketch e).

■ Brush glue on the back of the medallion. Press yarn with tassels around bottom edge of circle and bring the ends up to the top of the circle, extending over the top edge (sketch f). Place felt circle on back of medallion, over yarn, and press into place. Tie ends of yarn together at top of medallion and again near end of yarn to make a loop for hanging (sketch g.) Let dry.

■ With felt pen, draw a 2-inch (5-cm) circle on construction paper and cut out. Letter "Namsifu Mungu" on circle and glue to front of medallion.

Zungumza: **In Swahili, an African language, *Namsifu Mungu* means "I praise God." We can praise God by telling Him we think He is great. God likes to hear our praises to Him. Don't you like to be praised and told you're terrific? Hang your medallion where it will remind you to praise God.**

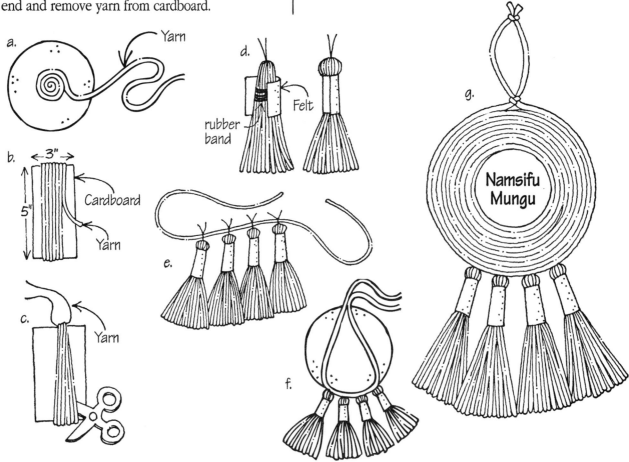

Reminder Chimes
(25-30 MINUTES)

Materials: Several colors of yarn, colorful wooden beads, pony beads, scissors, rulers. For each child—five random (6- to 9-inch [15- to 22.5-cm]) lengths of ³⁄₈-inch (1.875-cm) diameter dowels, one chenille wire.

Instruct each child in the following procedures:

■ String beads on the chenille wire and twist ends together to secure, shaping wire into a circle (sketch a).

■ Cut five 24-inch (60-cm) lengths of yarn.

■ Tie and knot one end of a yarn length around a dowel, leaving a 2-inch tail. Wrap long end of yarn around the dowel several times. Tie and knot again with the tail of the yarn (sketch b). Repeat for each dowel.

■ Tie dowels to the beaded wire at even intervals, leaving 8-inch (20-cm) tails of yarn (sketch c).

■ Gather all yarn ends together and tie in one knot (sketch d).

■ Trim ends of yarn as needed.

Enrichment Idea: Children paint dowels with tempera paint and allow to dry before assembling chimes.

Zungumza: What makes chimes move? (Wind.) **God is a little like the wind. We can't see God, but we know He is with us. When are some times you are especially glad to know that God is with you? Your "Reminder Chimes" will remind you that God is with you and you can talk to Him even though you can't see Him.**

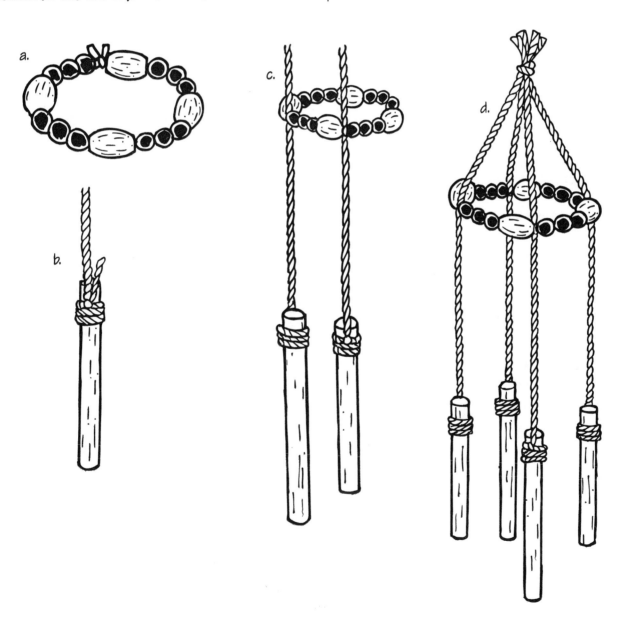

Wooden Notebook
(30-45 MINUTES)

▼▲▼▲▼▲▼▲▼▲▼▲▼▲▼▲▼▲▼▲▼

Materials: Leather scraps, ⅛-inch (.3125-cm) plywood, table saw, jute twine or leather lacing, scissors, sandpaper, brown acrylic paint and other assorted colors, water, paintbrushes, small plastic containers, clear acrylic spray, notebook paper, electric drill, ¼" drill bit, craft glue, newspaper.

Preparation: Cut plywood into pieces, three different sizes for each student: piece A—9½x11½ inches (23.75x 28.75 cm); piece B—1½x11½ inches (3.75x28.75-cm) and piece C—8x11½ inches (20x28.75-cm). In pieces A and B, drill holes that correspond to ruled paper (see sketch). Cover work area with newspaper. Thin brown paint (and other colors if desired) with water to use as stain. Pour into containers. Pour additional acrylic paint into containers.

Instruct each child in the following procedures:

■ Use sandpaper to sand wood pieces.

■ Brush the thinned paint on all sides of wood pieces. Let dry.

■ Paint words or design on front cover (piece C). Let dry. Spray with clear acrylic spray.

■ Place notebook paper between pieces A and B. Thread twine or lacing through holes and tie in front.

■ Cut leather pieces to use as hinges for front cover of notebook. Glue in place (see sketch). Let dry.

Zungumza: **You can use this notebook to record whatever you'd like—things that happen to you, events coming up, times you want to remember, prayers to God and answers to prayers. What will you write in your notebook?**

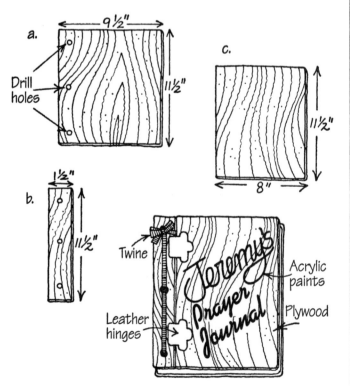

Jambo Giraffe
(30-45 MINUTES)

▼▲▼▲▼▲▼▲▼▲▼▲▼▲▼▲▼▲▼▲▼

Materials: Plaster of paris (one cup for each student), ¾-inch (1.9-cm) diameter wooden dowels, spoon, disposable container, water, orange, brown, and green acrylic paint, brown chenille wire, paintbrushes, small containers, plastic or silk greenery, glue, brown felt, ruler, newspaper, scissors, hand saw. For each student—two medium wiggle eyes, one 9-ounce (270-ml) plastic cup, one spring-type wooden clothespin. *Optional:* Small index cards, felt pens.

Preparation: With saw, cut dowels into 9-inch (22.5-cm) lengths and angle one end of each dowel—one dowel piece for each student. Cut chenille wire in fourths—one piece for each student. Cover work area with newspaper. Before class begins, mix plaster in disposable container following directions on package. Pour paint into small containers.

Instruct each child in the following procedures:

■ Paint the dowel and clothespin orange. Let dry.

■ Paint outside of the cup green. Let dry.

■ Paint the dowel with brown spots to resemble a giraffe's neck.

■ Fill cup with wet plaster and insert dowel in center, angled end up. Add greenery. Let plaster harden.

■ Glue center of chenille wire to center of clothespin behind spring (see sketch).

■ Cut two ears from felt and glue to clothespin.

■ Glue on wiggle eyes.

■ Glue the clothespin to the end of the dowel.

Enrichment Idea: Letter "Remember: God always listens to my prayers." on small index card. Insert card in giraffe's mouth.

Zungumza: **What do you think a giraffe might need to remember? (Where to find food, how to stay away from animals that might hurt him.) Your giraffe can help you remember things that are important, like how God loves for us to talk to Him every day.**

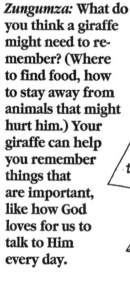

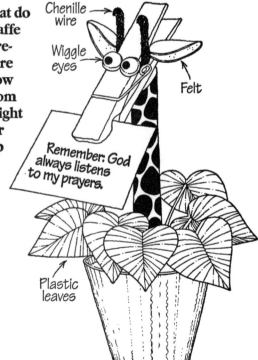

African Trading Bead Key Chain

(TWO-DAY PROJECT/50-60 MINUTES)

Materials: Air-drying or self-hardening clay, newspaper, bamboo skewers, acrylic paints, small paintbrushes, small plastic containers, masking tape, carpet thread, scissors, glue. For each student—a round metal key ring.

DAY ONE:

Preparation: Divide clay into 2-inch (5-cm) balls—one for each child. Cover work area with newspaper.

Instruct each child in the following procedures:
- Use clay to make beads in a variety of shapes and sizes. Make about 20-30½-inch (1.25-cm) beads.
- Push bamboo skewer through beads to make a hole. Thread several beads on each skewer (sketch a).
- If desired, scratch designs on the beads with the tip of another skewer.
- Allow beads to air dry on skewers.

DAY TWO:

Preparation: Cut thread into 12-inch (30-cm) lengths—two for each student. Pour paint into containers. Cover work area with newspaper.

Instruct each child in the following procedures:
- Paint beads on skewers a variety of colors. Let dry for several minutes.
- Place a piece of tape about 2½ inches (6.25 cm) from the end of each length of thread to stop beads.
- Remove beads from skewer. Put aside one bead.
- String the rest of the beads on the two threads. Stop stringing beads 2½ inches (6.25 cm) from the end of each thread.
- Remove tape from the thread and gather ends together, forming two loops of beads. Tie together (sketch b).
- Push all thread ends through the remaining bead (sketch c). Tie securely to key ring. Glue knot and trim ends.

Enrichment Idea: Make additional beads. Add more strands to key chain; make necklaces or bracelets.

Zungumza: In Africa, beads are used to decorate headbands and clothing. Earrings, necklaces and bracelets are worn by men and women. The beads are made out of shells, seeds, wood, aluminum, ivory and other natural materials. In one African tribe, the women wear many, many strands of beads to stretch their necks longer and longer, like a giraffe.

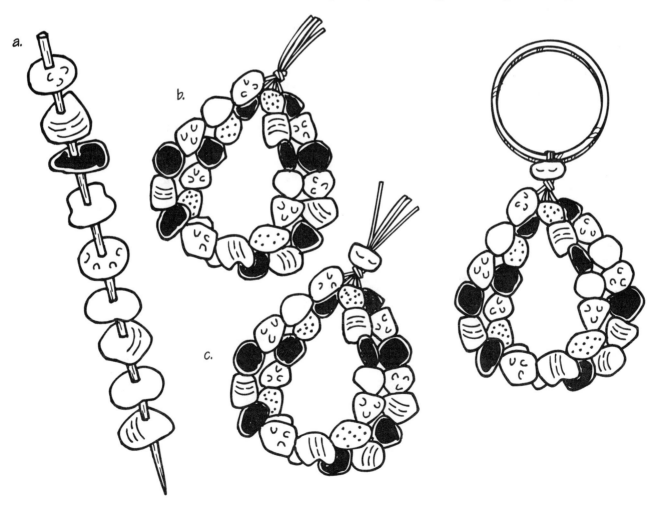

Lion Face
(TWO-DAY PROJECT/50-60 MINUTES)

▼▲▼▲▼▲▼▲▼▲▼▲▼▲▼▲▼▲▼▲▼▲▼▲▼▲▼▲▼▲▼▲▼▲▼▲

Materials: Lion Face Pattern, cardboard, pencil, tempera paints in yellow, brown, green, pink and black, clear acrylic spray, gold fringe, liquid detergent, lemon juice, thin brass wire, paper clips, measuring spoons, plastic knives, toothpicks, wax paper, thin paintbrushes, scissors, newspaper, ruler. For every two children—one bottle of white glue. For each child—three slices of white bread, one plastic container such as large margarine tub.

DAY ONE:

Preparation: Cut brass wire into 1½-inch (3.75-cm) lengths—six for each child. Trace Lion Face Pattern onto cardboard and cut out one for each child. Cut one 12x12-inch (30x30-cm) piece of wax paper for each child. Cover work area with newspaper. Place measuring spoons around table within reach of children.

Instruct each child in the following procedures:

■ Remove crusts from bread slices. Tear remaining bread into tiny pieces and place in plastic container. Add 3 tablespoons (45 ml) of glue, ½ teaspoon (2.5 ml) of liquid detergent and a few drops of lemon juice. Mix thoroughly with fingers until dough is smooth.

■ To make lion's face, place cardboard oval under wax paper. Shape one half of the dough into an egg shape, then place on top of the wax paper and flatten until it is the same size as the cardboard oval.

■ Use knife to score edges of lion's face to create mane (sketch a).

■ Form two small balls of dough and indent with thumb to make the ears. Attach to face with glue (sketch b).

■ Make a mounded teardrop shape for nose. Glue to face. Lightly press edges of nose into face to secure. Use toothpick to indent nostrils (sketch b).

■ Make three small balls for cheeks and tongue. Shape, flatten and glue on face. Insert pieces of wire into cheeks and bend back toward face to make whiskers (sketch b).

■ Make two small balls and flatten to create eyes. Glue onto face and use toothpick to make an indentation in each eye (sketch b).

■ Attach paper clip to back of face at top.

■ Allow to dry at least 12 hours.

DAY TWO:

Preparation: Cut fringe in 12-inch (30-cm) lengths, two lengths for each child. Cover work area with newspapers. Pour paint into shallow containers. Cover area outside with newspapers.

Instruct each child in the following procedures:

■ Paint lion face as desired. Place lion outside on newspapers to dry. Spray with acrylic spray.

■ Glue one length of fringe around edge of cardboard (sketch c). Glue the second length of fringe just inside the first. Glue lion face on top of fringe and cardboard. Allow to dry completely.

Simplification Idea: Use air-drying clay.

Enrichment Idea: Make faces of other African animals.

Zungumza: **Lions are known to be powerful and majestic. Often a lion is called the "King of the Jungle," but this isn't really true. Lions don't live in jungles at all—they live in open grassy plains in Africa called savannahs. And since female lions are much better hunters than the males, maybe a lion should be called "Queen of the Savannah."**

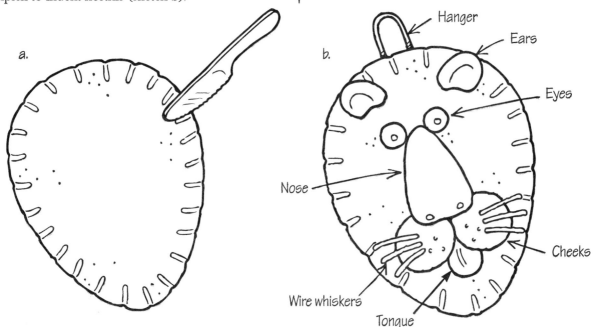

a.

b. Hanger Ears Eyes Nose Cheeks Wire whiskers Tongue

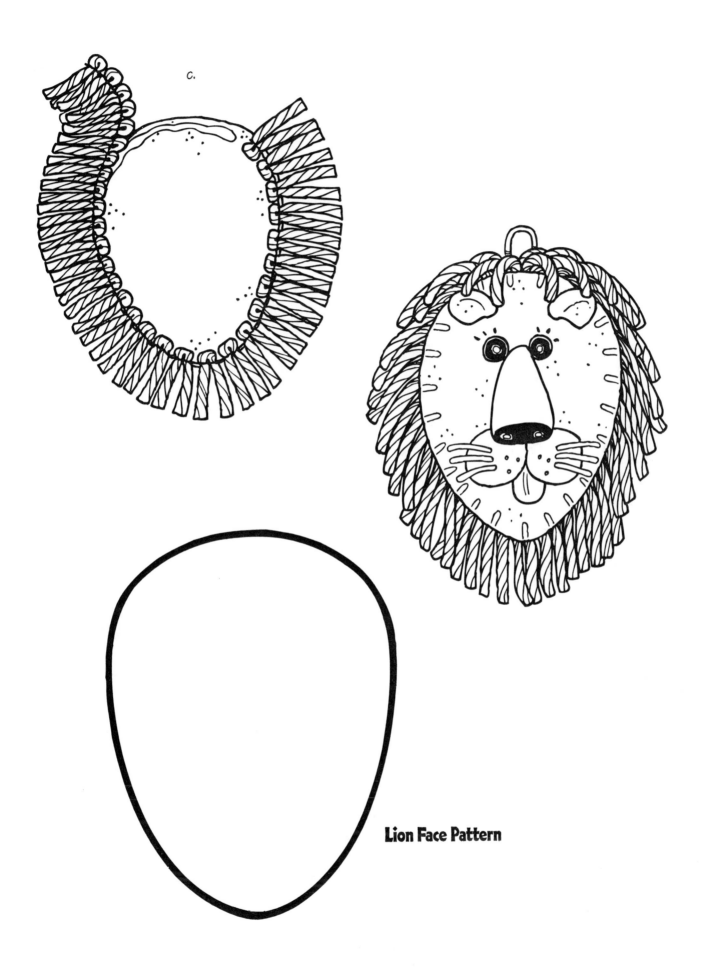

C.

Lion Face Pattern

Lord's Prayer Plaque

(20-30 MINUTES)

Materials: Lord's Prayer Pattern, photocopier, good quality paper, scissors, ruler, craft glue, braid, beads, feathers, yarn, shells, dried flowers and grasses, etc. For each student—one basket-type paper plate holder. *Optional:* Hot glue gun and glue sticks.

Preparation: Photocopy Lord's Prayer Pattern onto good quality paper—one for each student.

Instruct each child in the following procedures:

■ Cut out Lord's Prayer Pattern and glue onto basket.

■ Decorate basket with beads, braid, feathers, etc. and glue in place. NOTE: If using hot glue gun have an adult supervise gluing area.

■ Cut a 4-inch (10-cm) length of braid or yarn. Form into a loop and glue onto back of basket for a hanger.

Zungumza: **Who can say the Lord's Prayer?** Allow volunteers to say it. **Which is your favorite part of the prayer? Why?**

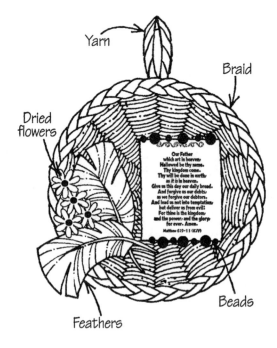

Yarn

Braid

Dried flowers

Feathers

Beads

Lord's Prayer Pattern

**Our Father
which art in heaven,
Hallowed be thy name.
Thy kingdom come.
Thy will be done in earth,
as *it is* in heaven.
Give us this day our daily bread.
And forgive us our debts,
as we forgive our debtors.
And lead us not into temptation,
but deliver us from evil:
For thine is the kingdom,
and the power, and the glory,
for ever. Amen.**

Matthew 6:9-13 (*KJV*)

Fabric-Covered Prayer Journal

(20-25 MINUTES)

Materials: Cardboard, a variety of fabrics in African or safari prints, butcher paper or self-adhesive paper, hole puncher, paintbrushes, shallow containers, newspaper, craft glue, craft knife, fabric scissors, pencils, measuring stick, sheets of writing paper. For each child—one metal two-prong paper holder with fasteners (available at stationery stores).

Preparation: Use craft knife to cut cardboard into 9x12-inch (22.5x30-cm) rectangles—two for each child. Cut additional cardboard into 1x9-inch (2.5x22.5-cm) strips—one for each child. Cut butcher paper or self-adhesive paper into 8½x24-inch (21.5x60-cm) rectangles—one for each child. Cut fabric into 11x28-inch (27.5x80-cm) pieces—one for each child. Cut fabric into 11x28-inch (27.5x80-cm) pieces—one for each child. Pour glue into shallow containers. Cover work area with newspaper.

Instruct each child in the following procedures:

■ With hole puncher make two holes at the top of one large cardboard piece 3 inches (7.5 cm) apart (sketch a).

■ Center butcher paper or self-adhesive paper on the cardboard with the longer end extending past the top of the cardboard (sketch b). With pencil, poke holes in the paper corresponding to the holes in the cardboard. Set paper aside.

■ Insert paper holder through holes in the cardboard and secure ends. Brush glue on back side of cardboard.

■ Brush glue onto one side of the other two cardboard pieces.

■ Lay fabric out, print side down. Place glued side of cardboard pieces onto fabric, leaving ¼ inch (.625 cm) between pieces (sketch c).

■ Brush glue onto outer edges of cardboard. Fold in corners of fabric, then fold edges of fabric over cardboard and press to secure (sketch c).

■ Poke the paper holder prongs through holes in the butcher or self-adhesive paper. Glue or press paper onto cardboard (sketch d). Secure ends of paper holder.

■ Punch holes in writing paper and secure inside journal using paper holder.

Zungumza: In Swahili, an African language, the word for prayer is *sala*. God understands the prayers of people all around the world no matter what language they speak. He can even hear our silent prayers and the prayers we write and keep in our journals.

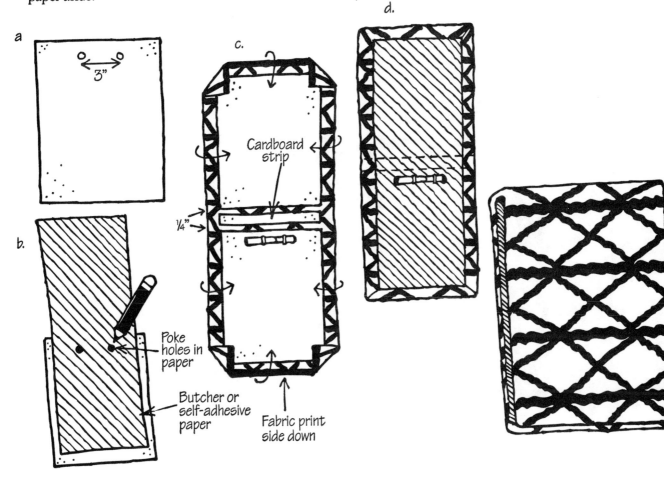

a

3"

b.

Poke holes in paper

Butcher or self-adhesive paper

c.

Cardboard strip

¼"

Fabric print side down

d.

Mankala Game Board

(ONE- OR TWO-DAY PROJECT/40-45 MINUTES)

Materials: Acrylic spray paint in a variety of bright colors, white mat board or heavy cardboard, craft knife, scissors, craft glue, black yarn, hole punchers, pony beads, fine-tip fabric paints in a variety of bright colors, measuring stick, dried beans or small pebbles, newspaper, Mankala Game Rules, photocopier, paper. For each child—one egg carton (non-Styrofoam type, dozen-size), two 9-oz. (270-ml) disposable plastic cups in primary colors, one plastic sandwich bag. *Optional*—a few extra egg cartons and plastic cups.

Preparation: Cut lids off of egg cartons. With craft knife, cut mat board into 16x4½-inch (40x11.25-cm) rectangles, rounding off the corners (sketch a)—one for each child. Cut plastic cups to a height of 2 inches (5 cm)—two for each child. Cut yarn into 5-foot (1.5-m) lengths—two for each child. Photocopy Game Rules—one for each child. Cover outside work area with newspaper.

Instruct each child in the following procedures:
DAY ONE

- Outside on work area, spray paint egg carton and mat board. Allow to dry.
- Punch holes around the top of each cup about ½ inch (1.25 cm) apart.
- Thread a length of yarn through one hole in cup and pull ends to meet. With yarn ends together, lace the edge of the cup (sketch b).

- When lacing is completed, tie yarn together in a knot near the cup. String one bead on each yarn end and knot ends together (sketch c).
- Repeat procedure for the second cup.
- Glue egg carton in the middle of the mat board.
- Glue the plastic cups on either side (sketch d).

DAY TWO

- Decorate the game board with fabric paints. Use lines, squiggles, dots and symbols to create African designs.
- Give each child 40 beans or pebbles for playing pieces. Two players need a total of forty pieces to play the game. Give each child a photocopy of game rules, and a plastic sandwich bag to hold game pieces and instructions.
- Explain how to play the game to the children and let those who are finished with their craft play with extra egg cartons, cups and playing pieces.

Zungumza: Mankala is a game that is played all over Africa. Sometimes Mankala boards are carved from wood or made from clay and are decorated with carved designs. But most often the game board is made by just scooping out holes in the sand and using rocks, shells or twigs for playing pieces.

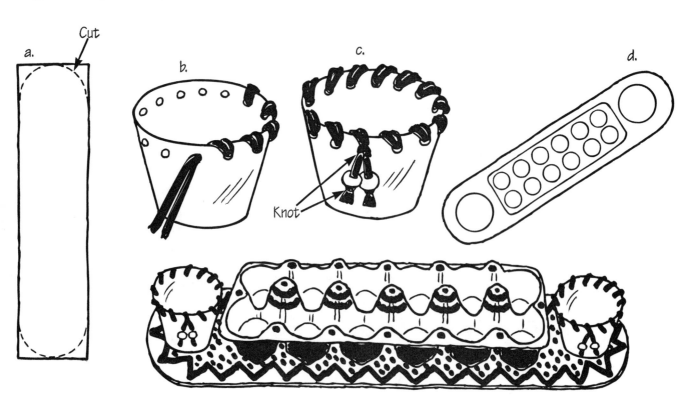

Mankala Game Rules

(Two Players)

1. Player B sets up the board by placing two to five playing pieces in each of the holes, using up all forty pieces (sketch a).
2. Player A starts by picking up all the pieces in his starting hole and dropping one piece into each hole moving counterclockwise (sketch a).
3. If the last hole now contains two or four playing pieces, Player A wins the pieces in the hole directly opposite and places them in his cup (sketch b).
4. Player A continues by picking up the pieces in his last hole and dropping these pieces into successive holes (sketch c).

5. Player A's turn continues around the board, taking the pieces from his last hole (whether or not he wins pieces) until he drops his last piece into an empty hole.
6. Player B then begins playing, picking up the pieces in his starting hole.
7. On each turn, players begin at their starting hole unless it doesn't contain any playing pieces. In this case, start at the first hole counterclockwise that does have pieces in it.
8. When eight pieces or less remain on the board, the game is finished. Players count up the pieces in their cups. The player with the most pieces is the winner.

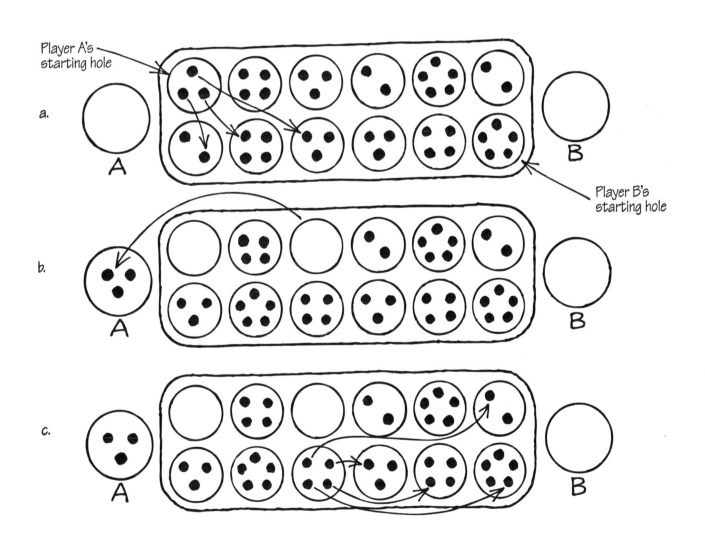

61

Savannah Diorama—Background Scene

(25-30 MINUTES)

Materials: Tree Pattern, tempera paint in a variety of colors (include blue, green, brown, white, yellow), paintbrushes, shallow containers, sponges, brown felt pens, glue, pencils, scissors, craft knife, newspaper. For each child—one large shoe box without lid, one sheet of brown or tan sandpaper.

Preparation: Cut off one long side of each box. Cut sponges in shape of Tree Pattern. (Damp sponges are easier to cut.) Cut sandpaper to fit the width and 1 inch (2.5 cm) less the length of each box. Cover work area with newspaper. Pour paint into shallow containers.

Instruct each child in the following procedures:

■ Sketch and paint savannah background scene (sky, flat land, sun, clouds) on the inside back and side panels of box (sketch a).

■ Dip sponge cut-outs into green paint to make trees. Use brown felt pen to make tree branches and trunks.

■ Cut a curvy diagonal line across sandpaper (sketch b).

■ Glue sandpaper onto bottom of box, leaving a curvy gap for a river (sketch c).

■ Paint river blue.

Zungumza: In Eastern African countries such as Kenya, a common tree is the acacia tree or thorn tree. Acacias give shade and food to many animals who live in the dry grasslands of the Serengeti region. Their leaves provide moisture for thirsty giraffes, and their low, spreading limbs give lions and leopards a place to nap.

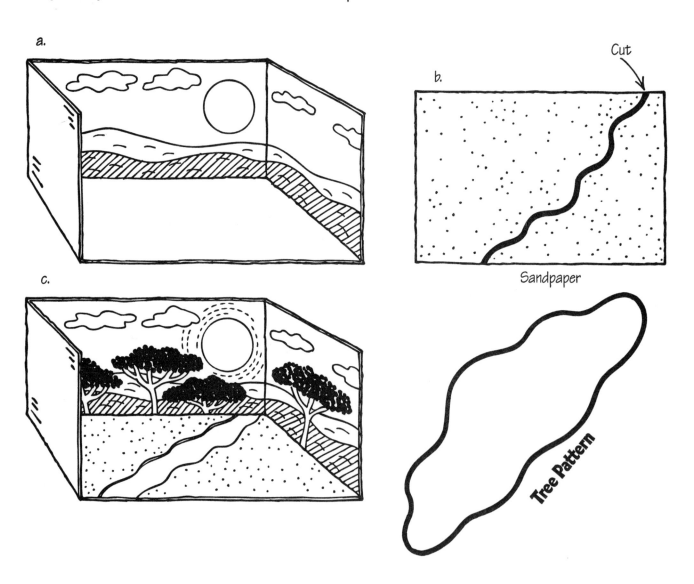

Savannah Diorama-African Hut
(25-30 MINUTES)

Materials: Air-drying clay, tan or yellow crepe streamers, tan construction paper, poster board, raffia, glue, tape, scissors, ruler.

Preparation: Cut construction paper into 4-inch (10-cm) circles—one for each child. Cut poster board into 8x2-inch (20x5-cm) strips—one for each child.

Instruct each child in the following procedures:

■ Cut small door in poster board strip anywhere along one long side. Shape strip into a cylinder and tape ends together (sketch a).

■ Pat clay out to about ½-inch (.625-cm) thickness. Wrap clay around cylinder and mold around door entrance and top and bottom edges.

■ Place in diorama (see page 62). Smooth bottom edge of clay onto sandpaper floor (sketch b).

■ Cut a slit to the center of the construction paper circle (sketch c). Overlap cut edges and glue in place to form a slight cone.

■ Place a line of glue around midpoint of cone. Glue a length of crepe streamer around bottom half of cone, making small folds to fit the cone (sketch d).

■ Snip bottom edge of streamer to make fringe.

■ Repeat above process for top half of cone.

■ Wind and glue a length of raffia around peak of roof (sketch e).

■ Glue finished roof onto top of hut (sketch e).

Zungumza: **In some small African villages, families live in simple huts made of mud, wood, grass or sticks. In some areas of the country, families build several huts arranged in a circle with a wall around them. Each parent has his or her own hut and the children sleep in a separate hut, where grain is also stored. A gateway hut is the only entrance into the family's home, and is also the guest room for visitors.**

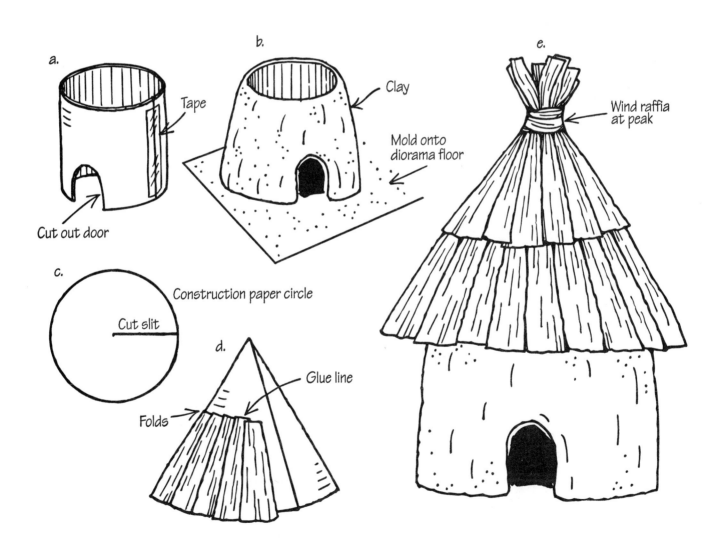

a. Tape / Cut out door

b. Clay / Mold onto diorama floor

c. Construction paper circle / Cut slit

d. Glue line / Folds

e. Wind raffia at peak

Peanut Monkey
(25-30 MINUTES)

▼▲▼▲▼▲▼▲▼▲▼▲▼▲▼▲▼▲▼▲▼▲▼▲▼▲▼▲▼▲▼▲▼▲▼▲▼▲

Materials: Tan or brown chenille wires, black fine-tip felt pens, craft glue, scissors, ruler, newspaper. For each child—two small wiggle eyes, one large paper clip, one single peanut in shell, one double peanut in shell, plus several extras.

Preparation: Cut chenille wire into the following lengths: ³/₄-inch (1.9 cm), 3-inch (7.5-cm), 5-inch (12.5-cm)—one for each child. Cut remaining chenille wire into 2-inch (5-cm) lengths—two for each child. Remove a few peanuts from shells and cut shells into monkey ears as shown in sketch a—two ears for each child. Cover work area with newspaper.

Instruct each child in the following procedures:

■ Open up paper clip and use end to poke a small hole in bottom of single peanut. Poke another small hole in top of double peanut (sketch b).

■ Squeeze a small drop of glue into each hole.

■ Insert one end of ³/₄-inch (1.9-cm) chenille wire into each peanut to join head and body (sketch c).

■ Use paper clip to poke holes for legs and tail. Squeeze small drop of glue into each hole.

■ Insert 2-inch (5-cm) lengths of chenille wire into holes for legs. Insert 3-inch (7.5-cm) length of chenille wire into hole for tail (sketch d).

■ Twist 5-inch (12.5-cm) length of chenille wire around neck to form arms (sketch d).

■ Glue ears and wiggle eyes onto head. Use felt pens to draw mouth and nose.

Enrichment Idea: Allow children the option of making elephants or cheetahs (sketch e). Decorate animals with poster paint and draw animal markings with felt pens.

Zungumza: **We often think that elephants like to eat peanuts, but in Africa they eat grass and dig up roots with their sharp tusks. To stay healthy they *need* to eat a lot of grass, although they might *want* peanuts as a treat. What are some foods that you really need to stay healthy? What do you most like for a treat?**

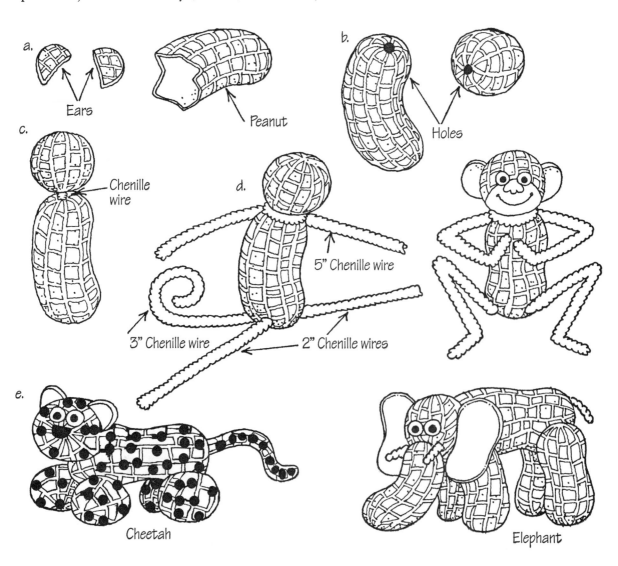

a. Ears Peanut
b. Holes
c. Chenille wire
d. 5" Chenille wire 3" Chenille wire 2" Chenille wires
e. Cheetah Elephant

64

Section Four

Reproducible Pages

Bible Memory Verse Coloring Posters

The following pages are reproducible and contain 10 Bible Memory Verse designs for younger elementary children and 10 for older elementary children. Ideas for using these pages include:

1. Use the photocopied pages as awards for children who memorize the Bible verse. They may take the page home to color and display.

2. Photocopy a set of coloring posters for each student. Cover with a folded sheet of construction paper and staple to make a coloring book.

3. Use the pages in class for transition times or for students who finish an activity ahead of other students.

4. Play a coloring game. Place a variety of felt pens on the table. Recite the verse together. Then each student may choose a pen and use it to color on his or her page for one minute. When time is up, students put pens down and repeat verse together again. Students then choose another pen and color for one minute. Repeat process until pages are completed or students tire of activity.

5. To customize pages, cover the Bible verse with white paper and letter another verse or saying in its place before you photocopy.

Student Certificates and Awards

The awards and certificates on the following pages may be personalized for various uses. Just follow these simple procedures:

1. Tear out certificate and letter the name of your program on the appropriate line.

2. Photocopy as many copies of certificate as needed.

3. Letter each child's certificate with his or her name (and achievement when appropriate).

Sticker Poster

1. Photocopy a sticker poster for each student.

2. After students color posters, attach them to a wall or bulletin board.

3. Students add stickers to their posters each day as they arrive. Or you may want to use stickers as rewards for reciting Bible memory verses, being helpful, or completing assignments.

African String Games

In Africa, string games such as cat's cradle have been used in storytelling for generations. Often the string figures correspond to a character or event in the story. Children will love to learn these slight-of-hand tricks to impress their families and friends!

To begin: Knot together a 5-foot (1.5-m) length of string or yarn.

Snapping Crocodile

1. Loop string across palms and behind little fingers and thumbs.

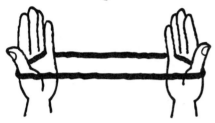

2. Reach across and slide right forefinger under the string that runs across left hand. Pull hands apart.

3. Repeat with other hand. Pull hands apart.

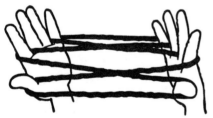

4. Have a friend place his or her hand into the crocodile's 'mouth' (between the string *X*'s).

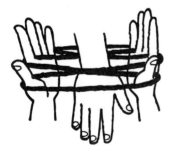

5. Drop strings from little fingers and forefingers. Pull strings taut to capture your friend's hand.

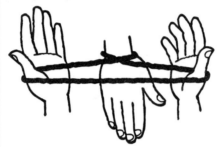

6. With hand still caught in string, loop string across palm and behind little fingers and thumbs. Repeat steps two and three.

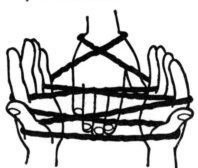

7. Have the friend push his or her hand through the string *X* from underneath. Release the strings from little fingers and forefingers and free your friend!

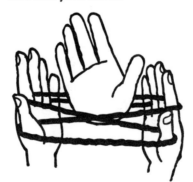

Lion Whiskers

1. Begin with steps one, two and three in Snapping Crocodile.

2. Drop string loops off thumbs.

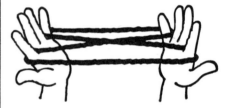

3. Reach thumbs under strings and hook the farthest string with thumbs.

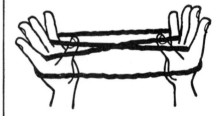

4. Pull thumbs back in position, pulling hooked string under other strings. Spread fingers apart.

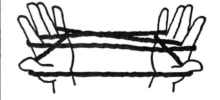

5. Without dropping the string, stretch thumbs over the second string and slide thumbs under the third string.

6. Pull thumbs, with third string, back into position.(You should have two loops on each thumb.)

7. Drop loops from little fingers.

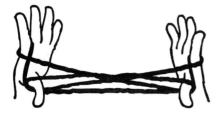

8. Stretch little fingers over the string that is closest to it and slide fingers under the next string.

9. Pull little fingers, with string, back into position.

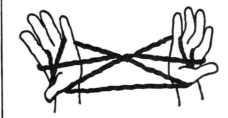

10. Drop all loops from thumbs. Spread hands apart to make Lion Whiskers.

The Mouse

1. Hang string loop over all five fingers of left hand. Spread fingers apart.

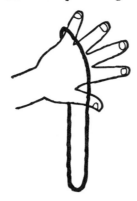

2. Pass right hand between left palm and the hanging string. With right forefinger, hook the string between left thumb and forefinger. Pull string down a few inches.

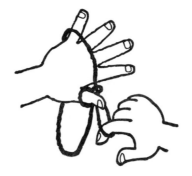

3. Twist pulled string around the string hanging from hand and place loop on left forefinger. Pull hanging strings gently to tighten loops on thumb and forefinger.

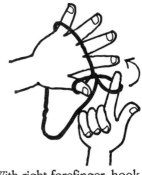

4. With right forefinger, hook the string between left forefinger and middle finger. Pull it down, twist around hanging string and place loop around left middle finger.

5. Repeat steps to place loops on remaining fingers.

6. Remove the loop from thumb. This loop is the 'mouse.' Pull the string next to the little finger. Continue pulling string to the right and watch the mouse 'run away' as each loop comes undone!

Front Paw Patterns

Lion Paper Bag Puppet

(15-20 MINUTES)

Materials: A lunch-size paper bag, white card stock, photocopier, felt pens or crayons, glue, scissors.

Procedure: Photocopy Head, Paw, and Tail patterns onto card stock. Cut out. Use felt pens or crayons to color cutouts. Glue head to flap of paper bag. Glue paws to sides of bag (see sketch). Glue tail to back of paper bag. Draw underside of lion on front of paper bag (see sketch).

Back Paw Patterns

Lion Head Pattern

Tail Pattern

Safari Animal Paper Chains

(10 MINUTES)

▼▲

Materials: Paper Chain Patterns, lightweight cardboard, pencils, large sheets of colored paper or animal print wrapping paper, scissors, felt pens or crayons.

Procedure: Trace Paper Chain Patterns onto lightweight cardboard and cut out several patterns. For vertical animals, cut paper into 5½x14-inch (13.75x35-cm) strips. For horizontal animals, cut paper into 3¼x22-inch strips. Fold a strip in half, then fold each half back to line up edges. Choose a pattern and center it on folded paper with edges on folds. Trace around pattern with pencil. Cut out animal through all thicknesses. Do not cut on fold line indicated on pattern. Unfold paper chain. Decorate with felt pens or markers if desired.

Fold

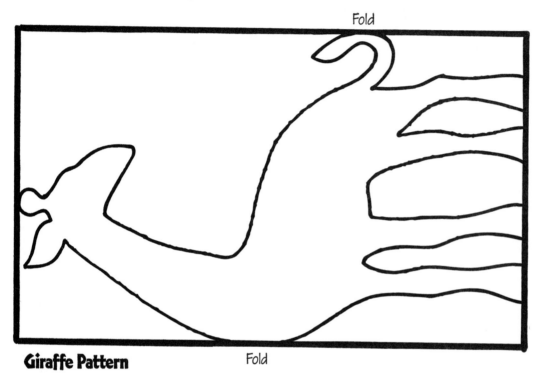

Giraffe Pattern   Fold

Fold

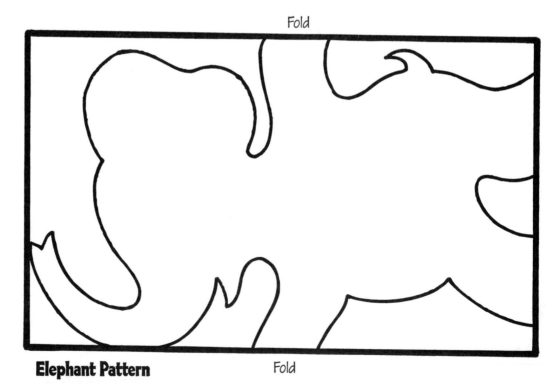

Elephant Pattern   Fold

70

Rhino Pattern

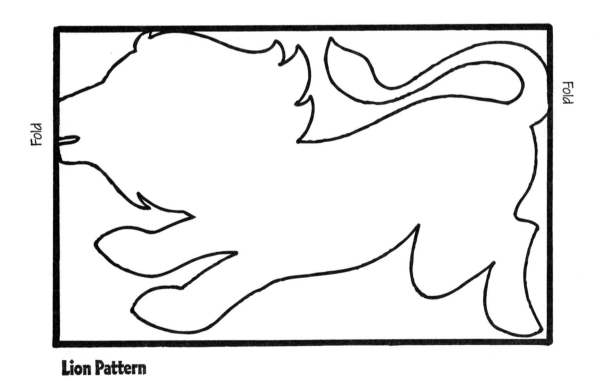

Lion Pattern

Fold

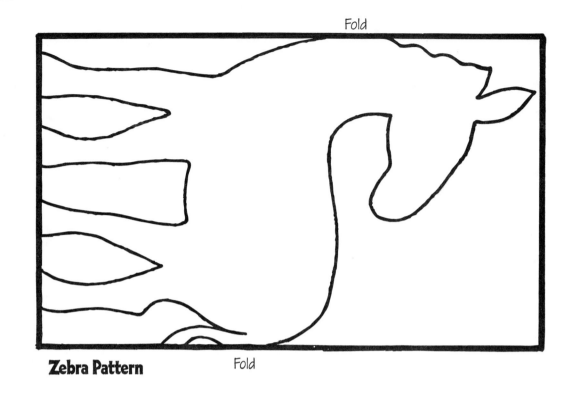

Zebra Pattern

Fold

Fold

Fold

Hippo Pattern

"Our Father which art in heaven,
Hallowed be thy name. Thy kingdom come.
Thy will be done in earth, as *it is* in heaven."

Matthew 6:9,10 (*KJV*)

"Give us this day
our daily bread."

Matthew 6:11 (KJV)

Orange

CHIPS

Younger Elementary Coloring Page 2

"And forgive us our debts, as we forgive our debtors."

Matthew 6:12 (*KJV*)

"And lead us not into temptation, but deliver us from evil."

Matthew 6:13 (*KJV*)

"For thine is the kingdom, and the power, and the glory, for ever. Amen."

Matthew 6:13 (KJV)

"Our Father which art in heaven,
Hallowed be thy name.
Thy kingdom come.
Thy will be done in earth, as it is in heaven."

Matthew 6:9,10
(KJV)

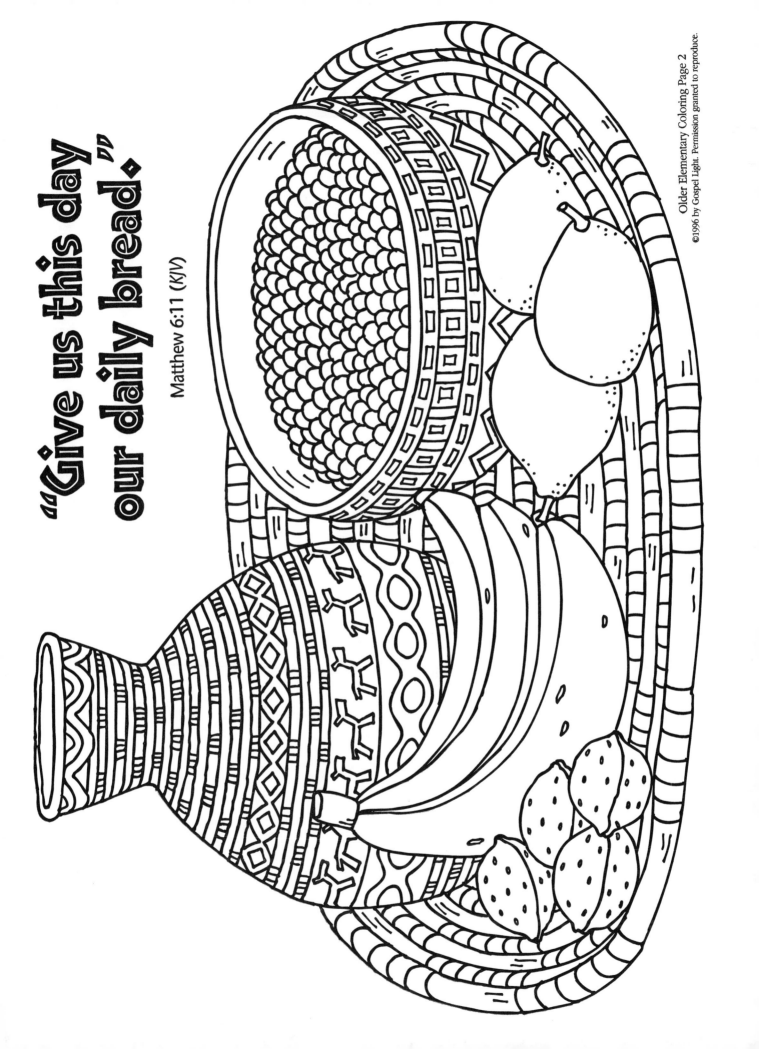

"Give us this day our daily bread."

Matthew 6:11 (KJV)

"FORGIVE us our debts, as WE FORGIVE our debtors." Matthew 6:12 (KJV)

Older Elementary Coloring Page 3

"And lead us not into temptation,

but deliver us from evil." Matthew 6:13 (KJV)

"For thine is the kingdom,

and the power,

and the glory, for ever.

Amen." Matthew 6:13 (KJV)

This is to certify that

_____

memorized all the Bible Memory Verses at

_____

thanks for traveling with us on our safari at

_____

Spotted Friend Award

_____

was spotted being a good friend at

_____

Visitor Award

_____

we're glad you joined our herd at

_____

Welcome!

Thanks for being
a safari guide.

This special award
is given to

FOR

Attendance Award

presented to

for attendance at

My Safari

Place sticker here.

Place sticker here.

Place sticker here.

Place sticker here.

Place sticker here.

Index